The Creation

*Shrushti, Incarnations of Vishnu,
Temples in the Himalayan Range,
Pilgrimage to Kedarnath and Badrinath*

T. Vanaja

ISBN 979-8-88704-310-4

DEDICATION

Dedicated to my parents Smt Sarala and
Late Sri Sannidhanam Sridhara Sarma

PRAYER SLOKA

I PROSTRATE TO THE DAWN/DUSK LAMP;

WHOSE LIGHT IS THE KNOWLEDGE
PRINCIPLE (SUPREME GOD);

WHICH REMOVES THE DARKNESS OF
IGNORANCE;

AND BY WHICH ALL CAN BE ACHIEVED IN
LIFE.

CONTENTS

PROLOGUE

My articles are usually based on my personal visits to spiritual places. I have extensively travelled the Indian sub-continent from north to south and from east to west. I have been to Sikkim, Guwahati, Nepal, Sri Lanka, Malaysia, Singapore and Cairo. I observed the architectural and spiritual aspects of these places. Here, I learnt about specific spiritual practices from sthala puranas. Some of my observations are from puranas I found through online and published sources. I've tried my best to write the truth clearly by explaining every aspect from puranas for easy understanding. In this book, two articles were published in Bhavan's Journal from Bharatiya Vidya Bhavan. They are Pilgrimage to Kedarnath and Badrinath in Oct issue 1914, Shrushti in 3 issues in Feb–March 1918. I hope the readers would be satisfied by the contents of the book.

– T. Vanaja

SHRUSHTI

SHRUSHTI means creation.

When, where and why?

It has been scientifically proven that our galaxy is one among infinite galaxies in the entire universe, and is one of the smaller galaxies. It has been proven that the Big Bang theory brought our solar system into being. The Big Bang theory is not the beginning of everything, just the start of the present cycle preceded by an infinite number of galaxies and will be followed by an infinite number. [When we watch the sky from our drawing room window or balcony, we usually find stars twinkling lightly which are billion light years away (A light year is the distance that light travels in one year in a vacuum which is 9.4607×10^{12}km = 9.46 trillion years) from our earth]. Mythologically (Hindu), the Brahma Vaivarta Purana (one of the Ashtadasa Puranas) states the same thing. The biggest galaxy is called "Gokulam" in which God resides in the form of light [Brahma Tejas]. In infinite galaxies (some small, some big), every galaxy had a God in the form of light. Our galaxy, which is smaller, also has God in the form of light [it is like villages, districts, states, countries, world].

WHY CREATION: Once upon a time, God (Brahma Tejas, decided to create a universe of living beings (Bhagavata Purana).

WHEN: Brahma Tejas started creation at the very beginning of the Universe.

WHERE: Creation was started by the Supreme Being as the sound "OM". Later the Supreme Being created Adi Parashakthi. Later, She created infinite galaxies and created life in the biggest universe. From then She was, and is, considered the Supreme Being.

Sri Devi Bhagavatam states that She (DEVI) is the original creator, observer and destroyer. She appeared as divine pure consciousness i.e., SHOONYA BINDU, the zero feminine energy. Satya Loka was located on her forehead. She created the universe with her hair; sun and moon from her eyes; the four directions from her ears; Vedas from her words; death, affection and emotions from her teeth, and Maya was manifested by her.

In the Vaishnava Puranas, Adi Parashakthi is depicted as the concept of Maya and Yoga Maya. Brahmanda Purana mentions that Adi Parashakthi divided herself into PURUSHA and PRAKRITI from a single seed.

The first seed gave birth to Lord KRISHNA [Supreme Being of Gokulam, biggest universe (He is not the Lord Krishna of Dwapara-yuga of 28th Vaivasvata Manvantara)] in masculine form, KALI in feminine form. Hence they are called cosmic siblings. Kali converted herself into LALITHA TRIPURA SUNDARI who gave birth to two bubbles. From one bubble arose Lord Vishnu and Goddess Gauri. From the second bubble arose Lord Shiva and Radha (who was Mulaprakriti, the consort of Lord Krishna of Gokulam).

Bhagavata Purana states that in the beginning, Lord Vishnu who was the principal of creation, preserver and dissolution (Brahma, Vishnu, Shiva) was the supreme 'HARI' (who is eternal). This was the supreme seed of all creations, subtler than the subtlest, greater than the greatest, larger than the largest. The Supreme has come to be considered as the womb of all objects.

In the very beginning (at the time of the original creation) the universe was in the shape of a golden egg and Lord Brahma, who was born from GOLDEN EGG was called HIRANYA GARBHA. Hiranya Garbha literally means GOLDEN WOMB or GOLDEN EGG which is poetically translated as UNIVERSAL GERM and is the source of creation of the universe. Brahma stems from the Sanskrit word "Brih" which means 'to grow' or 'to expand'. In puranic Hinduism, this is called BRAHMA and the Upanishads call it BRAHMAN. This egg split into two halves, the top half became the 70 Urdhva Lokas and the bottom half became the Adhara Lokas.

This completes the first stage of SHRUSHTI.

Lord Brahma of our universe has grown from the navel lotus of Lord Vishnu. In the Hindu Puranas, time calculations start with Lord Brahma's day which is called KALPA. Two kalpas constitute a day and night of Lord Brahma. In the puranas, a kalpa is equal to 4.32 billion years and is equal to 1000 maha-yugas. Each kalpa is divided into 14 manvantaras, each manvantara lasting for 71 yuga cycles (306,720,000 years). Preceding the first and last manvantara period is a juncture (sandhya), the length of Satya-yuga (1,728,000 years). In some books, it is written as 72 chatur-yugas approximately. A month of Brahma is supposed to contain 30 days or 268.2 billion years. According to the Mahabharata, 12 months of Brahma (360 days) constitute his year. His night also consists of 4.32 billion years. Brahma sleeps in his nighttime. 100 years of Brahma is the life cycle of the planet. The first 50 (pradhama parardhe = half the life span of 100 years of Brahma) years of Brahma are elapsed. Now we are in Shweta – Varaha kalpa which is the 51st (dvitiya parardhe = second half of 100 years of Brahma). At the end of every kalpa there usually is minor destruction in which all the living beings other than [Brahma, Vishnu, Shiva] die. When the destruction is over, creation starts afresh. At the end of every kalpa, there will be water everywhere in our universe [heaven, earth, underworld (patalam)]. Only the great Vishnu will sleep (rest) on VATA-PATRA [vata = banyan, patra = leaf] and he is called Vata Patra Sai.

OUR UNIVERSE: Growing from Vishnu's navel lotus, Brahma is the name of the PRINCIPLE which creates all realms (provinces). Before disappearing from Brahma's vision, Vishnu advised Brahma to focus upon him (Vishnu) and perform penance through which Brahma would be able to see all the worlds unfolded in his mind. In the beginning, Brahma had created four sages called Kumaras [Sanaka, Sanandana, Sanath Kumara, Sanath Sujatha], who are also called chatur-sanas (four sanas), and the great sage Narada from his thoughts. As a Kumara, Narada refused to procreate and took an oath of celibacy. Brahma created from his mind ten sons called PRAJAPATIS who are believed to be the fathers of the human race. Hence they are all called Brahma manasa - putras. The sons are 1. Sage Marichi 2. Sage Atri 3. Sage Angirasa 4. Sage Pulaha 5. Sage Pulatsya 6. Sage Kratu 7. Sage Vashishta 8. Sage Prachetasa 9. Sage Bhrigu 10. Daksha [there are several Dakshas]. The first nine sages had taken part in creation once only, they had not ruled the universe; they remained sages forever. Hence they are called NAVABRAHMAS. Daksha was not a sage, he took part in creation and ruled his subjects like a King. Hence he was called Prajapati (praja = subjects, pati = master). There were four types of beings that Brahma created through his mind power. From Brahma's thighs - demons (asuras), mouth - devas (suras), and sides - ancestors (pitris) were created. Humans came later. Demi-Gods like Indra and others (suras) were created from his mouth. From Brahma's age – birds, his chest - sheep and goats, his stomach and sides - cattle, his feet - horses, elephants, deer, camels, and from the hair on his body - plants were born. From Brahma's mouth - Brahmanas, chest - Kshatriyas, thighs - Vaishyas, feet - Sudras were born.

To continue with the process, Brahma gave birth to a man and a woman from his body. The man was named Svayambhu (self-manifestation) Manu and the woman was Shatarupa [she can take 100 (shata) forms (rupa)]. Humans are descended from Manu, hence they are called manavas. Brahma gave birth through his furrowed eyebrows on the advice of Shiva to Rudra (powerful). When Vishnu was sleeping two demons were born from his ears. One of them desired to have honey as soon as he was born, he was named Madhu (Sanskrit word for honey). The other one looked like an insect. He was named Kaitabah (The Sanskrit word for insect is "kita"). The demons fought with Brahma for a long time. Vishnu fought, killed them, and rescued Brahma. Hence Vishnu was named Madhusudhana ("sudan" in Sanskrit means to kill). After the demons were killed, the fat (medha) from their bodies formed the earth (our earth). Hence our earth is called "Medini" or "MEDHA".

Every Manu has a life span which is called Manu-antara or Manvantara. In his time he creates the world and all its species and, upon his death, Brahma creates another Manu to continue the cycle of creation. Vishnu takes a new incarnation and new demi-Gods and saptarishis are appointed. Brahma had created 13 Manus after swayambhu Manu. These 14 Manus [each Manu consists of seven rishis] and their respective Manvantaras constitute KALPA (a day of Brahma). At the end of each kalpa, there will be a period of dissolution (pralaya) and the world (earth, all the life forms but not the entire universe) will be destroyed and lie in a state of rest which will be called the 'night of Brahma'. In puranic Hinduism "OM or AUM" [pranava mantra] is the mystic name of the Hindu Trimurtis who represents the union of three Gods, i.e., A for Brahma, V for Vishnu, M for Mahadeva.

1. Manu was Swayambhu (self-manifested) Manu. The rishis were Marichi, Atri, Angirasa, Pulaha, Kratu and Pulastya. Vishnu had incarnated as Varaha in this Manvantara. Uttanapada was the son of this Manu. His son was Dhruva. Dhruva performed penance for Vishnu and was blessed with a boon that he (Dhruva) would be

placed in the sky as a star near the constellation of saptarishis and named "DHRUVA NAKSHATRA". According to modern science, the northern pole star "POLARIS" is the same as our "DHRUVA NAKSHATRA" and the constellation is called "URSA MAJORIS".

2. Manu was Swarocisha Manu. The rishis were Urjastambha, Agni, Prana, Danti, Rishabha, Nischara and Charvarivan.

3. Manu was Uttama Manu. The rishis were Kaukudini. Kurundi, Dalaya, Sankha, Pravahita, Mita and Sammita.

4. Manu was Tamasa or Tapasa Manu. The rishis were Jyothirdhama, Prithu, Kavya, Chaitra, Agni, Vanaka and Pivara. In this period Vishnu was named Hari as his mother was Harini, father was Harimedha— and he was also called Tapasa as he was born during Tapas (meditation). Gajendra - moksham event happened during this period.

5. Manu was Raivata Manu. The rishis were Hirannayaroma, Vedasri, Urddhabahu, Vedabahu, Sudhaman, Parjanya and Mahamuni. Varaha who appeared first in the Swayambhu Manu period stayed in the water till this

manvantara and killed Hiranyaksha the demon who ran away with earth.

6. Manu was Chakshusha Manu. The rishis were Sumedhas, Virajas, Havishmat, Uttama, Madhu, Abhinaman and Sahishnu. The Samudra Manthan event happened in this period.

7. Present Manu was Vaiwaswata Manu. The rishis are Kashyapa, Atri, Vashishta, Vishwamitra, Gautama, Jamadagni and Bharadwaja.

Usually, the rishis change for every manvantara.

Present manvantara's creation was started by sage Kashyap, son of sage Marichi and grandson of Brahma. He married 13 daughters of Daksha Prajapati. They are 1. Aditi 2. Diti 3. Ranu 4. Arishta 5. Surasa 6. Khasa 7. Surabhi 8. Vinata 9. Tamra 10. Krodhavasa 11. Ila 12. Kadru 13. Muni. Aditi's sons are 12 and are called Adityas. They are 1. Vishnu, 2. Tvashta 3. Aryama 4. Dhata 5. Vidhata 6. Shakra 7. Pusha 8. Vivasvana 9. Savita 10. Mitra Varuna 11. Amsha 12. Bhaga.

Diti's sons were called daityas. They were Hiranyaksha, Hiranya Kasipu and some powerful daityas like Bali, Vatapi, Maricha, and so on.

The hundred sons of Danu were called Danavas and they were cousins of Daityas and Adityas In the Danava line demons were born.

Arishta's were Gandharvas (singers of heaven). Surasa's sons were snakes, Khasa's children were Yakshas (demi-Gods) and rakshasas (demons). Surabhi's children were cows and buffalos.

Vinata had two sons named Aruna and Garuda. Later Garuda was made the king of birds and a vehicle (vahana) of Vishnu.

Tamra had six daughters—from these were born owls, eagles, vultures, crows, waterfowl, horses, camels and donkeys.

Krodhavasha had fourteen thousand children known as nagas (snakes). Ila gave birth to trees, creepers, shrubs and bushes.

Kadru's sons were also snakes among which Ananta and Takshaka were important. Ananta became the seat on which Vishnu reclines.

In Dhruva's lineage, Prachetas were born. They were not interested in ruling the world; they left for the forest to perform penance. There they created wind (Vayu) and fire (Agni).

When Kashyapa's wife Diti's son was about to be born (who was supposed to kill Indra), Indra sliced the baby in the mother's womb with his vajrayudha into 47 pieces. They were known as Maruts (They cried when Indra was cutting them into pieces and Indra shouted, "ma ruda" which in Sanskrit means "do not cry"). Though they were supposed to kill Indra they became his (Indra's) companions.

Further, Brahma had created Dharma, Kamadeva (Manmadha) and Agni from his heart, chest and eyebrows. Dharma comes from the Sanskrit word "dhri" which means "to support or bear" and means "path of righteousness". He married the ten daughters of Daksha. They were named Arundhati, Vasu, Yami, Lamba, Bhanu, Marudwati, Sankalpa, Muhurtha, Sadhya and Visva. Arundhati's children were objects (vishaya) of the world. Vasu's children were eight Gods called Vasus. Their names were Apa, Dhruva, Soma, Dhara, Salila, Anala, Prathyusha and Prabhasa. Anala's son was Kumara and he was known by the name Kartikeya as he was nurtured by Goddesses Krittikas. Prabhasa's son was Viswakarma who was the architect of the Gods. Sadya's children were Sadhya devas and Vishva's children were Vishwa devas. 27 daughters of Daksha were married to Chandra and known as Nakshatras. He (Dharma) later married another daughter of Daksha named Murti (ahimsa). Four sons were born to them. They were Hari, Krishna, Nara and Narayana [they were part (amsh) of Vishnu]. Hari and Krishna were engaged in Yogic Practice. Nara, Narayana went to Ganmadhan hills (presently called Garhwal – Himalayas) which are a part of the Himalayan mountain range, and performed penance from birth till today (they are chiranjeevis or immortal). There were many Daksha prajapatis.

When Brahma washed the holy feet of Vamana (incarnation of Vishnu in Vaivasvata manvantara), Ganga was born (washed water). As Ganga touches the lotus feet of Vishnu, she is known as Bhagavat Padi or Vishnu Padi. Brahma had created abodes: Kailasam for Shiva, Vaikuntam for Vishnu, Brahma Lokam for himself, Swargam (heaven) for Indra, Narakam (hell) for Yama, and Patalam (netherworld). As Ganga is Jalanabha [[(in Sanskrit jala = water, nabha = sky; water in the sky (cloud)] she remained in Brahmaloka. Sage Durvasa was born to sage Atri and Anasuya. He played a significant role in the current manvantara.

According to Maitri Upanishad, the universe emerged from (Tamas) darkness, first as passion (Rajas) which then refined into purity and goodness (Sattwa). The part which belongs to Tamas is Rudra, the part which belongs to Rajas is Brahma, and the part which belongs to Sattva is Vishnu.

After completion of creation, Vishnu started his duty as a preserver. In the present Vaivaswata Manvantara, Vishnu had transformed into ten important different forms (which are called avataras) to restore cosmic order. The first four avataras appeared in Satya or

Krita yuga (the first of the four yugas) also called 'The Golden Age'. They are Matsya, Kurma, Varaha, Narasimha (half-man / half-lion). The next three appeared in the second yuga which was Treta-yuga. The next two avataras appeared in the third yuga which was Dwapara-yuga and the tenth, the last one, will appear in the last yuga which is Kali-yuga. The average human lifespan was 100,000 years in Krita-yuga, in Treta-yuga it was 10,000 years, in Dwapara-yuga it was 1,000 years, and in Kali-yuga it is 100 years.

Some modern interpreters like the theosophist, Helena Blavatsky, in 1877 in the modern "Theory of Evolution" interpreted these avataras as:

1. Matsya – fish, the first class vertebrates (living in water)

2. Kurma – amphibious (living in both land and water)

3. Varaha – mammals, wild animals

4. Narasimha – beings that are half-animal and half-human

5. Vamana – short and premature human beings

6. Parasurama – early humans living in forests and using weapons

7. Rama – humans living in community, beginning of the civil society

8. Krishna – human practicing animal husbandry, politically advanced society

9. Buddha – humans finding enlightenment

10. Kalki – advanced humans with great powers of destruction

Radha, consort of Krishna of Gokulam expanded herself into Lakshmi, Saraswati and Ganga. Brahma with his consort Saraswati represents the Vedas, their spirit and meaning. They form the subject of many tales in Hindu literature. All knowledge, secular and religious, emanates from them and he resides in Brahma Lokam. Vishnu with his consort, Lakshmi, resides in Vaikuntam. Shiva with his consort, Parvati, [after the demise of his wife who was the daughter of Daksha Prajapati called Dakshayani, Shiva married Parvati (another form of Gauri from the bubble in the very beginning of creation), who was the daughter of King Himavant, born at the beginning of Vaivasvata (7) manvantara] resides in Kailasam.

Presently (this Kali-yuga) our supreme being created by "Brahma Tejas" is named BHUVANESHWARI who is one form of ADI PARASAKTHI [she has infinite forms (every Goddess is and was her form only)].

BHUVANESHWARI: Goddess (Eshwari) of the whole world or universe (Bhuvana) where worlds are tri – Bhuvana [bhuh (earth), Buvah (atmosphere) and Svah (heavens)]. The abode of Bhuvaneshwari is Mani - Dweepam. Hence she is called MANIDWEEPAVASINI (vasa = to reside).

This completes the second stage of SHRUSHTI.

'Ved' stems from the Sanskrit word 'vid' which means "to know". Hence Vedas means Knowledge, which is communicated by Lord Vishnu as Vyasa to humans so that humans would know how to live their lives and attain the objectives of human life. Vedas do contain information on all the knowledge that is needed to lead an ideal human life. Vyasa is a Sanskrit word that literally means compiler or writer. Vishnu incarnates as vyasa in every DWAPARA-YUGA and compiles Vedas. In this 28ᵗʰ Vaivaswata manvantara, the vyasa is Krishna Dwaipayana, who is chiranjeevi, [Krishna = black, dwaipayana = island - born, chiranjeevi = ever living] compiled puranas, Mahabharata and others. Vedas contain the knowledge of religious matters, medicine, astronomy, engineering, shipbuilding, flying saucers (aircraft = pushpaka vimana), nuclear weapons and computing. To help the human race in development, Vishnu had incarnated into some different forms as Dhanvantari (God of Ayurveda), who in turn incarnated as King DIVODASA. Susrusha was an ancient Indian physician and surgeon (plastic) which he learned from King Divodasa. He studied Dentistry, Obstetrics and Gynaecology. He authored SUSRUSHA—SAMHITA. CHARAKA (means wandering scholar) was the principal contributor of Ayurveda science in ancient India and authored CHARAKA—SAMHITA.

Bhagavata Purana (by Vyasa) explained the time scales starting from an atom (paramanu in Sanskrit) and explained the theory of relativity, quantum mechanics, concepts of superconductivity, plasma and nuclear weapons, electricity, chemistry, wireless, television, photography except for history and geography. Present weapons like Agni, Brahmos, rocket theory, etc., were all based on knowledge of ASTRAS like BRAHMASTRA, AGNEYASTRA, VARUNASTRA, and many more. The concepts of skyscrapers [harmyas in Sanskrit] and flying cities (Hastinapura) were also mentioned in the Vedas.

To know which form of the God the idol represents: Brahma is shown as sitting on a lotus flower holding the Vedas in his hands. Vishnu is shown with ten pairs of hands holding gada, shankha, chakra, and so on. Shiva as Lingarupa. All Goddess idols look the same unless they are identified by name. As Vishnu is the preserver, for material ambitions (worldly ambitions like job, money, etc.) people mostly worship different forms of Vishnu and different forms of Goddess Parvathi; Shiva is worshipped for siddi by sanyasis and sadhus.

Vedas contain religious ideas such as yagnas, homams, temple pujas, rituals and daily pujas for a perfect life. In temples, utsavams ["utsavam" is a Sanskrit word; ut = removal, sava = sorrow or grief] are performed for respective deities. Most humans are weak-minded, hence they need God's support. So they usually perform different pujas for different Gods in male and female forms. According to Hinduism, there are 33 crore Gods. They are all in different forms of the UNIQUE GOD manifested into different forms for different purposes (like President, PM, Cabinet ministers, state ministers, secretaries for all different departments, etc.). In Hinduism, idol worship is mostly practiced. In yagnas and homams for demi-Gods called ASHTADIKPALAKAS (asta = 8, dik = direction, palaka = ruler) [Indra, Kubera, Yama, Varuna, Eshanya, Agni, Vayu and Nairuti] (except eshanya = Shiva) and navagrahas [Surya (Sun), Soma (Moon), Mangala (Mars), Budha (Mercury), Brihaspati (Jupiter), Shukra (Venus), Shani (Saturn), Rahu (North Node: ascending node), Ketu (South Node: descending node) cannot be worshiped directly, they are to be invoked by mantras from RIGVEDA. To perform all these, idols have to be worshipped through SANKALPAM. According to Vedas, humans have to follow BRAHMA's CALENDAR.

Sankalpam.

Adya = first creator (Brahma); Adya Brahmane = During current Brahma's 51st year; dwitiya parardhe = in 2nd half (parardhe = half) of Brahma's 100 years; Swetha Varaha kalpe = in Swetha Varaha Kalpa (name of the first day of 51st year of Brahma).

Ashta Vimsathi thame, Kaliyuge prathama paathe [in the first (prathma) part (pathe) that comes for 28 time (astha=8, vimsathi = 20)].

Jambudweepe = In a place called JAMBUDWEEP which is part of the earth's seven parts. "Jambudweep" is a Sanskrit word meaning "island of jambu trees" (dweepam = landmass in water, island or continent, jambu = Indian Blackberry, jamun in Hindi). As per the Indian puranas, the entire landmass in the northern hemisphere was surrounded by the ocean in all directions. This giant landmass on earth was called Jambudweepam. This dweepam consists of modern Asia Europe, Africa and North America. Most of the South American continent, till the southern half of the African continent and entire Australia, was submerged under water.

Bharatavarshe = in Bharatavarsha. In ancient times India was called Bharatavarsha which expanded in the west including present Egypt, Afghanistan,

Balochistan, Iran and Sumeria up to the Caspian sea (this sea was called Kasyapa Samudra). This was called ancient Greater India.

Bharata khande = in Bharata continent. Bharata khanda refers to the Indian subcontinent which extends from the Himalayas in the north to Kanyakumari in the south.

Meroho dakshine parshve = to the south (dakshine) part (parshva) of Mount Meru. Presently Meru Peak (Mount Meru or Mount Sumeru) is a mountain that lies in the Garhwal Himalayas in the Uttarakhand state of India.

Shalivahana sahapte = In the times of King Shalivahana. King Shalivahana started the Saka era and the calendar is called Indian National Calendar or Hindu Saka Calendar. It began in 78 AD.

Asmin varthamaane vyavaharike = this (asmi) existing (vartamana) current period (vyavaharika). From here names of weekdays, months, years, dates, gotra (family of sage to which the person belongs) (except uttarayanam from Jan 13th or 14th to July 13th or 14th and dakshinayanam for the remaining six months by changing of sun's directions) has to be considered by different language calendars. It is a misconception that Brahma cannot be worshipped. Humans are following Brahma's calendar only. Every day, every puja, every person is uttering his name only; i.e. Adya Brahmane.

Humans are following and maintaining the Vedic rules set by GOD till now. Hope future generations continue to do the same.

This completes the third stage of SHRUSHTI.

Conclusion:

This article is an attempt to clear the doubts and misconceptions about persons involved in the events in Hindu mythology. The timeline for the Brahma age is massive. It is very hard to understand. Most of us are confused about whether all the events in Hindu mythology happened. I am confidently writing in this article that all the events "really happened" but in different timelines and with different people with the same names. We have to understand that all the names of rishis, Indra, Daksha, and so on are repeated several times in every manvantara and kalpa. At the end of Brahma's 100 years, our universe will be completely annihilated. Then once again our universe will be created. Another Brahma, Vishnu and Shiva will be recreated. Once again the cycle of creation will start. It is understood that Brahma, Vishnu, Shiva, Manus and other Gods and demi-gods are all posts only (like President, PM, and so on).

The cycle continues.

HUMAN INCARNATIONS OF LORD VISHNU

Lord Vishnu had innumerable incarnations. No purana has mentioned the exact clarification of the time period of incarnations of Vishnu. According to Bhagavata Purana, Lord Vishnu is the supreme who was the principal of creation (Brahma), preserver (Vishnu), dissolution (Shiva). Brahma's hundred years make one cycle. Infinite cycles have elapsed. Even in the first years of Brahma's present cycle, the number of Vishnu's incarnations are unknown. The present period is the 51st (Shweta Varaha kalpa) year of Brahma's 100 years (humans follow Brahma's calendar, which consists of 268.2 billion years) cycle. As Brahma's timeline was and is massive, it is obscure (unknown) how many forms Vishnu might have incarnated. Whenever needed in whichever form, Vishnu had incarnated to earth in that particular form. Though the Dasa Avatars of Vishnu are famous, the puranas state that the remaining 14 incarnations which are Narada, chatur (4)-sanas, Nara - Narayana, Adi Purusha, Kapila, Dattatreya, Yagya, Rishabha,

Prithu, Dhanvantari, Mohini, Hayagreeva, Vyasa and Balarama are also important in this present cycle.

The earth was formed from the fat of demons Madhu and Kaitabha [who was in the form of an insect (kita in Sanskrit), both emerged from Vishnu's ears (Sri Devi Bhagavatam)] when killed by Vishnu. These were the first creatures of evolution. Vishnu as Brahma created chatur - sanas, Narada. As they refused to procreate, Brahma created nine rishis (Nava Brahmas) and Daksha Prajapati. To continue the process of creation, Brahma created 14 manus. In the 1st manvantara named Swayambhu Manvantara, Vishnu incarnated as Varaha. No incarnations occurred in the 2nd, 3rd and the 4th manvantaras. In the 5th manvantara, Vishnu as Varaha who appeared in the 1st manvantara stayed in the water, reappeared in the 5th manvantara, and killed Hiranyaksha. As the Samudra-Manthan episode occurred in Chakshushi, the 6th manvantara, Kurma, Dhanvantari and Mohini incarnations appeared at the time of the Samudra-manthan. Vishnu might have incarnated as Narasimha in this manvantara. Some puranic experts presumed that incarnations of Vishnu occurred in some Chatur- yugas and some assumed that they occurred repeatedly in every Chatur-yuga (no purana explained the exact manvantaras of incarnations). The timeline in Krita-yuga was massive; the physical structures of mammals (Meena, Kurma,

Varaha and Narasimha), demons and humans were enormous.

Life (humans, reptiles, birds, etc.) started in Vaivasvata manvantara only by sage Kashyap. According to western experts, mammals (dinosaurs, lizards, etc.), existed billions of years ago, which is in comparison to manvantaras of Hinduism. The lifespan of humans was 1,00,000 years in Krita-yuga. Scientifically proven that human existence might have started 40,000 years ago approximately in the Dwapara-yuga of the present 28th Chatur-yuga of Vaivasvata Manvantara. The first animal with a human gene, called NEANDERTHAL after the gorilla, was quite big. Over the years the size of humans has reduced to the present size.

The first dynasty was called Surya Vamsha, as the 7th Manu Vaivasvata was the son of Surya. Another dynasty Chandra vamsha was started by Chandra, grandson of Brahma, and son of sage Atri and Anasuya. Ikshvaku (Ikshvaku literally means sugarcane) was the son of Vaivasvata and he ruled the Kosala kingdom in Satya-yuga of 1st Chatur-yuga of Vaivasvata Manvantara. He was the 1st king who executed Manusmruti (religious rules composed by his father Manu). After King Ikshvaku ruled the Kosala kingdom, the dynasty was called the Ikshvaku dynasty. It is known that Sri Rama belongs to the Surya Vamsha, Pandavas and Kauravas of Mahabharata belong to the Chandra Vamsha. King Sagara was born in the Ikshvaku dynasty in Satya-yuga of 3rd or 4th Chatur-yuga. He had 60,000 children who were burnt to ashes by sage Kapila (Kapila was an incarnation of Vishnu and the founder of the Samkhya philosophy of Hinduism). King Bhageeratha was the great-grandson of King Sagara. He might have been born in the Treta-yuga of the 7th Chatur-yuga and ruled the kingdom for many years. His main aim was the salvation of the souls of his 60,000 ancestors.

King Mahabali or Bali, who was the grandson of Prahlada learnt bhakti and righteousness from his grandfather and expanded his kingdom even to heaven, and ruled righteously for several chatur - yugas (unsure of number). On the request of Indra, Vishnu incarnated as Vamana (dwarf brahmin boy) in the 7th Chatur-yuga and suppressed Bali to patala (netherworld), which was more prosperous than heaven, making him immortal. When Vishnu as Vamana asked for and was granted three paces of land at the time of Aswamedhayaga; Vamana stepped one foot on earth and, with the other foot, made a hole in the shell of the heavenly universe causing a few drops of water from the spiritual world to spill into our universe. These sacred, divine, pure, rare drops are called Ganga. As Ganga was born by the touch of Vishnu, she is called Vishnupadi and

Bhagavatpadi; she was residing in heaven as a cloud (Ganga is jalanabha, jala = water, nabha = sky).

As King Bhageeratha wanted to bring Ganga down to earth for the salvation of his ancestors' souls, he performed penance to Brahma to release Ganga and performed penance to Shiva to hold her in his Jatajutham, as the earth could not bear her pace. After Ganga was released from jatajutham of Shiva, who had changed his place from Kailasam to the Himalayan mountain range in north India (then Bharat, hence the name Mt. Kailash), to Gomukh or Gaumukh (gau = cow, mukh = face) which is the terminus of Gangotri glaciers and the source of the River Bhagirathi, and from there the river flows through Gangotri which is the origin of Bhageerathi River (as it was brought by Bhageratha, here it is called Bhageerathi) joins with Mandakini (calm), Alaknanda and Devprayag to form the Ganges River.

Whenever too much violence prevails, to spread peace in the world, Vishnu incarnates in a peaceful form in every Brahma's Kalpa (day). In the Treta-yuga of the 8th or 9th Chatur-yuga, Vishnu incarnated as Rishabhadev who started Jainism. According to Jain cosmology (the science of origin and development of the universe), $10^{\wedge}1631$ ($10 \times 10 \times \ldots 1631$ times) does not have a temporal beginning or end. Its universal history divides the time cycle into two halves named Avasarpini and Utsarpini with six aras (spokes) in each half cycle and the cycle repeats endlessly. In every half-cycle, 24 tirthankaras appear and the first among them would usually establish Jainism. In the present time cycle, Rishabhanatha was credited as the first tirthankara who was born in the present Avasarpini ara. Jina means knower (enlightened person). Though Rishabhdev belonged to the Ikshvaku dynasty and was king of Ayodhya for some years and enjoyed life with his wife and hundred children, the sudden death of one dancer from heaven triggered him to renounce his kingdom, family and material wealth to become an ascetic. He went to Mt. Ashtapad which is approximately 7 km from the famous Mt. Kailash in the Himalayan mountain range, practiced meditation for a thousand years (the lifespan of humans in Treta-yuga was 10,000 years), and attained enlightenment to start Jainism. He preached Jainism for many years and attained moksha in Mt. Ashtapad.

According to Garuda Purana, Brahma Purana and Sattwata Samhita, Vishnu incarnated as Dattatreya to start and spread Guru bhakti in the Treta-yuga of the 10th Chatur-yuga, to a pious couple—sage Atri and his wife, Anasuya. According to some other puranas, he was the incarnation of three forms of NARAYANA (Brahma, Vishnu, Maheshwara). According to puranas, most of the incarnations occurred at the foot of the Himalayan mountain range only. Dattatreya might have been born in the present-day Kashmir jungles near Amarnath temple. He left home at a very young age to lead a monastic life. Though he was born in North India, he is more popular in the west (Gujarat), Maharashtra, Andhra Pradesh and Karnataka in South India. He is revered as Adi-Guru (first-teacher). Upanishads, Avadhuta gita (song of free) are attributed to Dattatreya. Philosophy of Dattatreya is present in Dattatreya Upanishad (tantra-focussed), in Darshana Upanishad (yoga-focussed), Avadhuta Upanishad (written by Dattatreya on principles of Advaita Vedanta) and Sandilya Upanishad (text on yoga). He is mentioned in Jabala Upanishad, Narada Parivrajaka Upanishad and Bikshuka Upanishad. Yajnavalaka Upanishad mentions Dattatreya's name in the path of renunciation. He is mentioned in Mahabharata and Ramayana. He is immortal and presently he is meditating in the Gandhamadhana mountains (presently Garhwal - Himalayan mountains).

Vishnu incarnated as Parashurama (parashu in Sanskrit means axe, who holds an axe in hand) in the 19th Chatur-yuga to slay all the evil kings on the earth. Though he was born before Rama and Krishna, he appeared in Mahabharata, Ramayana. According to Bhagavata purana, he served as a mentor to Bhishma,

Drona and Karna. As he is immortal, presently he is living in the Mahendra mountains (part of the eastern ghats mountain range in Odisha).

The most important incarnation of Vishnu is Rama. Vishnu incarnated in the 24th Chatur-yuga as Rama. He was portrayed as the perfect son, the perfect father, and the perfect king. The purpose of this incarnation was to set characteristics of an ideal person for humans. He was, is, and forever will be a role model for human beings for billions of years ahead. He was a perfect human being. As Vishnu had to slay Ravana-Brahma (a demon king) he had to incarnate in human form and be born to the pious couple, king Dasaratha and Kausalya of the Ikshvaku dynasty, who ruled the Kosala kingdom.

Ravana-Brahma was the son of sage Vishravasu (son of sage Paulatsya who was one of the 10 prajapatis or Brahma manasaputras) and the Daitya princess, Kaikasi, (daughter of demon king Sumali and Thataka). As Kaikasi wanted an exceptionally powerful heir, she married sage Vishravasu and gave birth to a ten-headed baby named Dasagreeva, also called Dasaanana (dasagreeva = dasa + greeva = 10 + neck, dasaanana = dasa + aanana = 10 + face). He was a staunch devotee of Lord Shiva. As he could not satisfy Lord Shiva though he performed penance for so many years, he started chopping off his head and every time he did, by the grace of the Lord, a new head arose thus permitting him to continue the penance. Thus pleased by effort, Shiva granted him celestial nectar of immortality which would be stored in his navel. Lord granted him some more boons such as supremacy over three worlds (devas, serpents, etc.) (except nara and vanara) and 10 severed heads. Hence the name Dasamukha (dasa + mukha = 10 + faces = 10 faces) or Dasaanana (dasa + anana = 10 + faces = 10 faces) or Dasagreeva (dasa + greeva = 10 + necks = 10 necks. As he became more powerful by these boons, he went to Kailasa (abode of Shiva) to conquer his benefactor. Having become blind with ego, he started turning mountains with his toes. Then Shiva became angry, pressed the mountain top with his toe, and Ravana's toes got stuck under the mountain. As he could not bear the pain, he started screaming loudly, then the Lord appeared before him and named him Ravana ("ravana" in Sanskrit means yelling loudly). As Ravana is half Brahmin, he is called Ravana Brahma and half asura, he is called Ravanaasura (Ravana + asura).

By the order of Lord Shiva and Parvati, celestial architect Vishwakarma built a beautiful city with gold named Lanka Puri (island city). It was presented to Vishravasu (the Brahmin who performed the house-warming ceremony as Dakshina) and Vishravasu transferred it to Kubera (Vishrava's son by another wife and half-brother of Ravana Brahma) and later on it was usurped by Ravana. As Ravana ruled tri-bhuvanas for 14 chatur - yugas and Ramayana occurred in the 24th chatur - yuga, it is understood that he might have been born in the 8th or 9th or the 10th Chatur - yuga. Ravana was a great scholar and learnt all the four Vedas. He also learnt astrology and authored "Ravana Samhita".

The archaeological department had proved that 10 million years ago, Sri Lanka was at the same distance from the present Indian sub-continent. According to Valmiki Ramayana, Lanka Puri which was ruled by Ravanaasura was quite vast and might have spread from present Sri Lanka to present Indonesia. Valmiki Ramayana states that Hanuman leapt 100 yojanas (1 yojana = 8 miles) from the tip of the southernmost part of India to Lanka which is not the part of present-day Sri Lanka. Most of Lanka (later named Ravana Lanka) was submerged in the Indian ocean. Present-day Sri Lanka is called Vibheeshana Lanka as Lord Rama crowned Vibheeshana as the king of Lanka before the war. The Archaeological department proved that the war was fought a million years ago in this part of the land, Rama Setu was built, footsteps were of Hanuman (big, small), Indrajith's nikumbh yagna's place (My visit to Sri Lanka) which are presently existing in this part of the land was of Ramayana's period. Satellite pictures proved the presence of Ram Setu which is presently called Adam's bridge. Not to disturb the sacred Ram Setu, ships travel from the Bay of Bengal to the Arabian sea circumventing Sri Lanka. Indonesians still believe the war between Rama and Ravana was fought in present-day Indonesia

As Ravana was a staunch devotee of Lord Shiva, he used to worship 1 crore shivalingas in a single day (presently one day in Kali-yuga has 24 hours, but one hour in Treta-yuga= 3× one hour in present Kali-yuga) travelling by pushpaka vimana belonged to Kubera (Ramayana). When Ravana was ruling Lanka, there was a natural formation of a hill in Go (cow) - karna (ear) form. Ravana's mother was unhappy about not being able to worship Lord Shiva on Gokarna hill. To please Lord Shiva, Ravana tried to cut a hill with his sword and the hill was cut into Tri-kon (three angles). The Lord was pleased by the devotee and presented him with a shivalinga which is named the Trikoneswara linga. Once when Ravana tried for an atmalinga of Shiva, the Lord gave him one linga as he (Ardhanaareshwara) could not give an atmalinga without consulting his consort, Parvati. That linga was drowned in the ocean but was brought back and installed near Ravana cut. Once again Ravana did rigorous penance to Shiva and Parvati for the Lord's atmalingam. He was blessed with it on one condition that lingam should not be put down on the earth. As he was bringing the lingam down to earth from Kailasam, it was put down on the earth by Vigneshwara at a place named Gokarna (presently in Karnataka, southwestern India). The Lord here is called Mahabaleshwara lingam. It is understood that there are two Gokarnas on planet earth.

In the Trikoneshwara temple, Lord Shiva's consort is installed as Shankari Devi. She is the first of ashtadasa shakti peethas. Sati Devi, daughter of Daksha Prajapati was born and married Shiva (against the wishes of Daksha) in swayambhu manvantara. Having been insulted by her father Dakshaat the Daksha Yagna, she immolated herself. Shiva, grief-stricken by this, went to the forest with her half-burnt body. Troubled by this lord Vishnu cut Sati Devi's body into 108 parts with his Sudarshana Chakra. Of which 52 pieces fell on the Indian subcontinent (present India, Pakistan, Bangladesh, Nepal, Sri-Lanka, Bhutan) of earth, and the remaining fell on other planets, except on the Sun. After submerging, and re-emerging at the end of every yuga, Chatur-yuga, all the Shakti Peethas and Jyotirlingas are found by the sages at present places. Sati Devi was re-born as Parvati and married Shiva at the beginning of Vaivasvata Manvantara (Shiva Purana).

Not only a devotee of Lord Shiva, but Ravana was also a Brahma-Jnani. According to the Bhagavata Purana,

Jaya and Vijaya were gatekeepers of Lord Vishnu's abode, Vaikuntam. There were cursed to be born on earth by chatur-sanas for their refusal to permit them to enter Vaikuntam. Lord Vishnu amended the curse in two ways. They could be born as devotees of Vishnu seven times or three times as enemies of Vishnu. They chose the second option as they could not live without the Lord's presence. First, they were reborn as Hiranyaksha and Hiranyakasipu; their second birth was as Ravana and Kumbhakarna and their third birth was as Shishupala and Dantavakra. Though they were born as demons and portrayed as wicked, they were Brahma - jnani (ब्रह्म - ज्ञानिन्). They waited patiently with enmity for several chatur-yugas (most of the demon rulers had ruled tri- bhuvanas for 14 Chatur-yugas), for the Lord to appear and slay them.

In this birth as a demon, Ravana ruled his kingdom very well and his subjects were very happy with him. To reach Lord Vishnu he could find only one way which was to abduct Vishnu's consort Goddess Lakshmi who was shakti. As to reach her was quite impossible, Ravana wanted to abduct Vedavati who was a form of Goddess Lakshmi born to Lord Vishnu's devotee King Kushadhwaja. Some legends state that Vedavati immolated herself when Ravana approached her while she was performing penance, later he took the ashes to Lanka. On seeing the ashes, Mandodari, wife of

Ravana, ordered the servants to bury the ashes. They buried the ashes in King Janaka's Mithilapuri (presently it is on Nepal and India border), where she was born as a girl when King Janaka was ploughing the field. Hence the name Sita (line of ploughshare).

Goddess Lakshmi descended to earth first as Vedavati. As Lord Vishnu knew the future, he incarnated as Rama (In the name Rama, Ra is taken from the Ashtakshari Mantra: "OM NAMO NARAYANAYA", "ma" is taken from the Panchakshari Mantra OM NAMA: SHIVAYA. Hence, the Rama mantra is more powerful as SHIVAAYA VISHNU ROOPAYA, SHIVA RUPAAYE VISHNAVE), and was born to Dasaratha and Kausalya as their first-born son. He acquired all knowledge required to be a king from sage Vishwamitra and married Sita in a swayamvar by lifting (breaking) Shiva Dhanus gifted by Lord Shiva to King Janaka. Ravana also participated unsuccessfully in this swayamvar. Though Ravana was a devotee of Lord Shiva, he could not lift the Shiva Dhanus. Humiliated, he vowed to abduct Sita Devi. As he could not touch Sita Devi (he was fully aware that she was Goddess and he should not touch her), he abducted her from Chitrakuta mountains (presently in Madhya Pradesh, they spread from MP to AP). Meanwhile, on the way to Lanka, Ravana killed Jatayu (vulture). Sita threw her jewels down on Kishkinda Aranya (presently it is a region on the banks of the Tungabhadra River near Hampi in Karnataka— then it was called Pampa Sarassu where Hanuman rested). When they reached Lanka, Sita was held captive in Ashokavana under the Shishumpa tree as Sita Devi refused to stay in Ravana's palace. Ravana used to visit Sita Devi every day at Brahma Muhurta (Brahma Muhurta is the time of Brahma, one hour and thirty-six minutes before sunrise precisely and is called "creator's hour") to take her blessings (excerpts from the pravachanam on Shodashi in Telugu compiled by Sree Gunturu Seshendra Sharma).

Lord Rama with Lakshmana travelled south in search of Sita Devi and met Vanara king, Sugreeva, and Hanuman in Kishkindaranya. Having met Rama, Hanuman found his idol and went to Sri Lanka in search of Sita Devi. Hanuman returned after finding Sita Devi in Ashokavana. Rama built a stone bridge with the help of the vanaras (Nala and his brother Nila were credited with building Rama Setu) from Rameshwaram in India to Talaimannar in Sri Lanka, which was the shortest distance between the two countries then and now. Before travelling to Lanka, sage Agastya who was kumbhasambhava (kumbha + sambhava = pot + born = born in pot) appeared before Rama and imparted ADITYA HRUDAYA STOTRAM. Before crossing the bridge Rama installed a Saikata (sand) lingam on the banks of the ocean in Rameshwaram and prayed to Lord Shiva. In Lanka, Rama killed Kumbhakarna, Indrajit and Ravana. As Ravana possessed a thorough knowledge of Ayurveda and Political science, he taught these two to Lakshmana before his death by the order of Rama and attained moksha. To ward off Brahma Satya dosha, Rama installed another saikata lingam in a place presently named Manavari in Sri Lanka. After the death of Ravana, Sita Devi was brought to the war zone and was asked to prove her sanctity by entering the fire. Immediately Agni brought the real Sita Devi from the fire (Sita's agni pravesa sthalam) and took Maya Sita in. Rama was then pleased and installed two more shivalingas to ward off Brahma hatya dosha and crowned Vibheeshana as the king of Lanka and awarded him the boon to be immortality. He then returned to AYODHYA with Sita, Lakshmana, and others in Ravana's Pushpaka Vimana. He ruled the country for approximately 11,000 years (the life span of humans in the Treta-yuga was 10,000 years) and then ascended to Vaikuntam. Sita Devi gave birth to twins named Lava and Kusha in Valmiki's ashram. Later she sent them to Rama (Sita Devi did not return to Ayodhya from vanavasa) and ascended to Vaikuntam before Rama. She descended to earth much earlier than Rama and left the earth much earlier than Rama. Ramayana was, and is, the story of

Sita Devi, who suffered so much to ward off the curse of her devotees Jaya and Vijaya.

At the end of every Dwapara-yuga Lord Vishnu incarnates as Vyasa (title) and compiles puranas till that day. Literally, vyasa means a writer. In every Chatur-yuga, vyasas had different names. In this 28th Chatur-yuga, the vyasa was named Krishna Dwaipayana (Krishna means dark complexion, dwaipayana means island born, dwaipa = islander, ayana = arrival; here it means born). Not only was he the compiler of Mahabharata, but Vyasa was also a character in it. He is considered to be one of seven immortals still in existence.

Another important incarnation of Lord Vishnu was Krishna. This incarnation took place almost at the end of Dwapara-yuga (the human life span in Dwapara-yuga was 1000 years). According to Brahma Vaivarta Purana and the Big Bang theory, there were, are, and will be infinite universes. In the present cycle, the biggest universe in the galaxy is called Golokam, and our universe is a smaller one. The purpose of this incarnation was for Lord Vishnu to participate in the Kurukshetra war, and the Vishnu of our universe (every universe has its own Brahma, Vishnu and Shiva) granted the wishes of rishis to dance with him. As Vishnu could not attend both at the same time, he requested Lord Krishna (this Krishna is different from our Krishna) of Golokam to be born on our earth. Lord Krishna of our earth was the amsh of Golokam Krishna and Vishnu of our universe (excerpts from Harivamsam, pravachanam by Kurtala peethadhipati). Lord Krishna was born to Devaki (sister of Kamsa, king of Mathura) and Vasudeva (son of Yadava king, Shurasena, was the cousin of Nanda who was chief of Gokul mandal) as the eighth son with the seventh son, Balarama, (who was also considered as amsh of Vishnu).

Though he was born in jail in Mathura, he was brought to Gokul in fear of getting killed by Kamsa. Goloka Krishna's consort Radha Devi was born in a village near Gokul (not to be confused with another Radha who was Krishna's aunt and a staunch devotee of Krishna). As the purpose of this incarnation was to slay evil and demons, Krishna started killing them as an infant and this continued till he was 11 years old. Meanwhile, he played with gopalas and gopikas (rishis) as promised, on the river banks of Kalindi River (presently Yamuna River). He showed Yashoda 14 worlds and liberated the gandharvas from the curse. Approximately at the age of 12, Goloka Krishna with Radha Devi and gopikas left for Vrindavan to participate in Raasa Leela for Lord Brahma's one day (kalpa) which is 4.32 billion solar years and Gokula Krishna went to Mathura, killed Kamsa—left Shishupala and Dantavakra as he had promised his aunt not to kill them till they completed 100 cases of abuse against him, and ruled Mathura for approximately 50 years.

Jarasandha, King of Magadha (presently Patna, Nalanda and Gaya), attacked Mathura (he was Kamsa's uncle) and was defeated by Krishna 17 times. As Jarasandha was destined to be killed by Bheema, Krishna and Balarama left Mathura unseen by Jarasandha and hid in the city, Kushasthali (presently Muladwaraka in

Kodinar village approximately 36 km from present Somnath in Junagarh district of Gujarat, India). As Krishna set his first foot here it was called Muladwaraka. On Krishna's orders, Vishwakarma, architect of devas, built the city of Dwaraka in one night on the seashore. Originally the same landmass was a sports ground for King Raivata who ruled Kingdom Anartha in the 5th manvantara, named Raivata Manvantara. It was spread in the Raivataka mountains (presently Girnar mountains) and submerged in the ocean. The same landmass was brought back and Dwaraka ("dwaraka" in Sanskrit means "many doors") was built, which also was called DHARAVATI. Present Muladwaraka is the small landmass that remained when the entire Dwaraka was submerged. Some land mass also remained by the sea shore which is presently called "Bet Dwarka" ("Bet" in Gujarati means island). This is where Krishna met Sudhama when Sudhama visited Dwaraka. Sudhama's birthplace was Porbandar and it is near Bet Dwarka. Historians believe that the original Dwaraka may have extended from present-day Dwarka to present-day Somnath.

DWARKA TEMPLE

Yuddhistara, eldest of the Pandava brothers, having become king of Indraprastha (present-day New Delhi) performed the Rajasuya yagna. Krishna helped Bheema in killing Jarasandha (king of Magadha). At the Rajasuyam, when Yuddhistara and his four brothers were honouring Krishna, Krishna had to chop off the heads of Shishupala and Dantavakra (when they completed a 100 cases of abuse), with his Sudarshana chakra. Later he visited Nanda and Yashoda and showed them Goloka Brundavanam by Divya Vimana. Krishna assisted the Pandavas whenever and wherever they needed him. He ruled

Dwaraka totally for 75 years. After the Mahabharata war, Yuddhistara ruled Hastinapur (approximately 100 km from present New Delhi) for 36 years, crowned Parikshit [son of Uttara and Abhimanyu, (son of Arjuna and Subhadra)] as emperor of the Kuru kingdom, and left on a pilgrimage with his four brothers and wife, Draupadi. Krishna ruled Dwarka for 36 years (having been cursed by Gandhari and the saptarishis for the complete annihilation of the Yadavas) and went to Balka teerth (near Somnath temple at Prabhas teerth where the confluence of Hiranya, Kapila and Sarasvati meet the Arabian sea).

He left his physical body when an arrow shot by a hunter, Jara, hit him, and he finally departed for Vaikuntam. Present-day Dwaraka was built by Viswakarma in the period of Krishna's great-grandson Vajranabha (son of Aniruddha) on a landmass of 12 yojanas left when the original Dwarka was submerged. According to SURYA SIDDHANTA (a Sanskrit treatise on Indian astronomy), Kali-yuga started at zero hours on 18 Feb 3102 BCE which is also considered the date of Krishna niryanam from earth to Vaikuntam. Krishna lived on the earth for 125 years which was a very young age as the lifespan of humans in the Dwapara-yuga was 1000 years (all the years mentioned are different from the Kali-yuga).

After the Mahabharata war, once again Lord Vishnu wanted peace to prevail across the earth. He incarnated as Siddhartha Gautama at the beginning of the present Kali-yuga (6-5 BC). He belonged to the Ikshvaku dynasty. Gautama's mother queen Maya is believed to have conceived him near the legendary lake ANAVATAPATA in Sanskrit and ANATHOTA in Pali, which is presently called Manasasarover (created by Lord Brahma's mind). Hence the lake which was part of the Himalayan mountains is very sacred to Hindus, Buddhists and Jains (Rishbhanath attained moksha here). Gautama was born in Lumbini (presently in Nepal) and raised in Kapilavastu (Northern Indian Frontier), the Sankya capital. He was believed to have lived from 6th to 5th BCE. He was not interested in material life from childhood, yet he was forced to marry and bore a child named Rahula (Gautama named him Rahula as he was an obstruction to his ambition to be a sanyasi). After he became Buddha he took Rahula as his first disciple), went to Gaya (Bihar, India), and meditated rigorously under the pipal (Bodhi or Aswatha which is very sacred for Hindus) tree, received enlightenment after seven years. After enlightenment, Gautama's name changed to Buddha which means enlightenment. Lord Buddha followed

Ahimsa which means not to hurt any living beings. Buddhism spread from present-day AFGHANISTAN through the complete Himalayan mountain range to CHINA, FAR EAST, JAPAN, and was more popular there. He manifested in the form of the mantra "OM MANI PADME HUM" which is a six-syllable Sanskrit mantra. Buddha went to mahasamadhi at the age of 80 around 544 BCE.

Generally, Lord Vishnu incarnates for the destruction of evil forces, to impart knowledge, and to establish dharma. According to the Varaha purana, Lord Vishnu descends to earth in search of his consort Goddess Lakshmi (she was angry when sage Bhrugu hit Vishnu's chest with his foot, which was the place of Lakshmi Devi). According to another legend Vishnu descended on earth to marry Padmavati as she was Vedavati in Ramavataram (Rama could not marry Vedavati as the purpose of Ramavatara was to have only one wife) and to satisfy Yashoda's (Lord Krishna's adopted mother in Dwapara-yuga, born as Vakula Devi in present Kali-yuga) wish to perform Vishnu's marriage. Vishnu sheltered in Varaha Kshetra as this was the place on earth where Vishnu as Varaha stayed. After marriage to Padmavathi, a rift between Lakshmi and Padmavathi broke out, Lord turned into a stone idol with shanka, chakra, gada, and Lakshmi on his chest, and was installed in Tirupati, Andhra Pradesh (India). It is unsure whether this incarnation is a human incarnation or not, but he will bless the people till the end of Kali-yuga.

End of 1st part.

The world is moving very fast with computers, laptops, and mobiles with the latest technology like the internet, WIFI, android, IOS, Windows, and so on. What are android and Windows? A computer is just a machine created by humans; it understands only machine language i.e. 0,1. It operates on a set of instructions called software. Android and Windows are called operating systems (unlimited to humans) that run the entire global system. But the biggest operating system is the SUPREME GOD who controls the entire galaxy with unlimited, infinite, eternal, endless power, and to whom people are like laptops and mobiles.

After God created human beings, he gave a set of instructions to humans which are called Vedas. God taught humans to worship unseen power (God) through singing. Saama Veda is the root of music with seven swaras. The Rig Veda mantras were rendered by using swaras in Samagana. Svara (note in the musical scale) added to Rik (praising) mantras is "Saama". In the word "Saama", "Sa" means Rik and "ama" means svara. Rik or svara in isolation does not constitute Sama. The union of the two alone is Sama. Music has no geographical border. The word music is explained as M = melody, U = universal, S = soul, I = individuality, C = cultural development. It says if a person worships with this music, the person reaches God. Historically, it was proven that humans existed for approximately

40,000 years before they created music with musical instruments like drums, bells, wooden flutes, etc. Over the years music has developed; many different musical instruments were created, and classical music like Hindustani and Carnatic was developed by composers like Thyagaraja swamy, Swati Thirunal, Jayadev, Meera Bai, and more.

ANANTA PADMANABHA SWAMY,
THIRUVANANTHAPURAM

According to the sthala purana of Ananta Padmanabha Swamy temple in Thiruvananthapuram, Lord Vishnu incarnated as Ananta Padmanabha here around 5000 years before. In this temple, Lord Vishnu incarnated as Padmanaabha (padma = lotus, naabha = navel) reclines on Ananta (adisesha), his right hand is placed over the shivalingam; two consorts, Sridevi and Bhudevi by his side; Brahma emerges on the lotus which emanates from Vishnu's navel. This shows SAMPOORNA

TATTWA OR PARIPURNA TATTWA of Lord Vishnu. According to the regional literature of Kerala, the land of Kerala was formed by the land brought out of the sea by Parashurama. Lord Rama is worshipped in one and only one form as Rama with Sita, Lakshmana, and Hanuman everywhere, whereas Lord Krishna is worshiped in different forms in Vrindavan (UP), Mayapur (WB), Puri Jagannath (Odisha), Dwaraka (Gujarat), Pandharpur (Maharashtra), Udupi (Karnataka), Nathdwara (Rajasthan), Guruvayur (Kerala) which are in India.

According to Sthala Purana of Guruvayur temple, Lord Krishna selected a place for an idol which he was worshipping (even God has to worship one form of God when he incarnates as a human being) to be installed by Guru and Vayu after his niryana and before Dwaraka submerged into the sea. Hence the name Guruvayur. This temple is in Guruvayur Kshetra which was built by Vishwakarma immediately after Krishna niryanam approximately 5000 thousand years before. Narayana Bhattathiri (1560-1646 AD) who was an eminent scholar in astronomy, mathematics had compiled his greatest masterpiece NARAYANEEYAM (1036 slokas), consisting of the dashavataras of Lord Vishnu by composing 1 dasaka (10) slokas daily in sanctum sanctorum of Guruvayur temple and completing 1036 slokas in approximately 100 days. Alwars are poets who wrote poetry about Lord Vishnu, Lord Rama and

Lord Krishna. Alwar means one who floats in deep love towards Vishnu and his incarnations. Basically, alwars were 12 (most of them are Tamilian) saints who popularized Vaishnavism in South India. Goddess Andal is the only female alwar among 12 alwars. They praised DIVYA DESAMS (108 abodes or temples of different forms of Lord Vishnu) with 4000 slokas compiled as a book called NALARIYA DIVYA PRABHANDAM by Nadamuni a 10th-century theologian. Of the 108 divya desams 105 temples are in present India, the 106 temple is Muktinath (place of liberation) in Nepal, 107 is Milk Ocean, and Thirupaalkadal (thiru = auspicious, paal = milk, kadal = sea) in Tamil, 108 is Paramapadam (Vaikuntam). Nammalwar composed verses on Krishna, and Chera (Malayala) King Kulasekhara Alwar (9 AD) composed verses on Rama and Krishna. Andal, a female alwar, had composed 30 verses (pasurams) imagining Sri Ranganatha Swamy of Srirangam (Tamilnadu) as Krishna, and these pasurams are recited daily one in the dhanurmasam period (Dec 15th to Jan 13th or 14th every year) in all Vaishnava temples (she is the incarnation of Goddess Lakshmi). Kulasekhara Alwar also compiled the famous MUKUNDA MALA stotram about Krishna imagining himself as Devaki (mother of Krishna) in Sanskrit. The famous KRISHNA KARNAMRUTA (karna + amruta = nectar to ears) was composed by poet Bilwamangala Thakur (13-14 AD) also called LEELA SUKA, in Sanskrit. He also composed BALA-

MUKUNDA ashtakam, GOVINDA - DAMODARA stotram in Sanskrit. Sage Vyasa compiled DAMODARA stotram in padma purana.

Though Adi Shankara born in Kaladi in Kerala lived for 32 years in 8 AD was a staunch sanyasa. A devotee of Lord Shiva, he composed many stotras on Lord Vishnu as well. Some of them are: Bhajagovindam, Achyutashtakam, Krishnashtakam, Govindashtakam, Lakshmi Nrusihma pancharatnam, Dasavatara stotram, Panduranga ashtakam, Narayana stotram, Jagannatha ashtakam (Some believe that Jagannatha ashtakam was written by Chitanya Mahaprabhu of Mayapur in WB, whose follower, Sri Prabhupada, started ISCON, and some believe it was written by Sree Nidamarri Sarvamangala Sastry, a Telugu brahmin from Puri at the beginning of the 19th century) and Kanakadhara stotram. He had described the Lords in each stotra differently. Composers like Sadasiva Brahmendra, Vutukkadi Venkata kavi (Tamilnadu), Narayana Thertulu, Siddhendra Yogi (united AP) and Vyasaraya (Karnataka) composed krutis mostly on Lord Krishna. Thyagabrahma, Bhadrachala Ramadasu, Purandara Dasa, Deekshitar and Swati Tirunal composed mostly on Lord Rama, Lord Krishna. Saint Annamacharya composed krutis mostly on Lord Venkateswara, Lord Krishna, Lord Rama and Lord Narasimha. It is understood that all the composers composed songs on different incarnations of Lord Vishnu. Chandrasekhara Swamigal of Kanchi Kamakoti peetham worshipped Lord Krishna as Amba (excerpt from pravachanam). Ramashtakam was composed by Sage Vyasa, and Sri Rama Raksha Stotram was composed by Brahmarishi Vishwamitra which was recited to him in his dream by Lord Shiva.

Ramanuja Charya presented the importance of devotion to personal God (means Lord Vishnu). He is famous for VISHISHTADVAITA (qualified non-dualism) and he was inducted into Vaishnavism. He wrote the bhashya on BRAHMA SUTRAS and the BHAGAVADGITA. He presented epistemic (the knowledge) and soteriology (study of religious doctrines of salvation) importance of the Bhakti movement.

UDUPI, KARNATAKA

In Udupi (Karnataka), when the great saint, Madhwacharya (whose followers are called Madhwas), was trying to compose DWADASA STOTRAM sitting on the seashore, Balakrishna's idol covered in sandalwood paste was found by him. Later, he installed the idol in the temple and composed the stotra with 12 names. In Udupi, the Lord's idol completely turned towards a side window in the sanctum sanctorum when an untouchable named Kanakadasa was not allowed the darshan of the Lord. The Lord turned to the side where Kanakadasa was standing and allowed the devotee to have his darshan. Here devotees have their darshan from the window which is named Kanakana Kinkini. Kuchipudi dance ballet BHAMA KALAPAM by Siddhendra Yogi, completely based on Lord Krishna, was revived in 1930 AD by an American dancer named Ester Sherman (later changed to Ragini Devi). Bhakta Jayadev (12 AD) who belongs to Odisha compiled GEETA GOVINDAM in Sanskrit about Radha Krishna's Raasa Leela. Vidyapati (14-15 AD) of Bihar composed Radha Krishna Leela in Brajubuli (Mythili) language (Mythili was the language used in the Mithila kingdom ruled by King Janaka). Naamdev, Tukaram, and Gnanadev composed songs in Marathi (Abhang) and Sanskrit. Jnanadev translated Vyasa's Bhagavadgita in Marathi named JNANESHWARI. Tansen (16 AD), one of the Navaratnas in Akbar's court was a musician, composer and vocalist who composed songs on Krishna and Narayana in Brij Bhasha (Yadava language).

Narsi Mehta, a Gujarati Vaishnavite belonging to Junagadh in Saurashtra, composed 22,000 kirtans on Raasa Leela when he was taken to Vrindavan and shown the entire Raasa Leela of Krishna with gopis by Lord Shiva. His bhajan VAISHNAVA JANATO was a favourite of Mahatma Gandhi and is a prayer song in Sabarmati Ashram. According to Bhavishyottara Purana, Tulasidas (16 AD) was the incarnation of Sage Valmiki in Kali-yuga. He compiled Ramacharitamanas in the Awadhi language which was the language of the land at that time and a dialect of Hindi. Ramacharitamanas is the shorter version of Valmiki Ramayana (It consists of 24,000 slokas). Tulasidas composed 61 slokas on Krishna in Brij Bhasha when he visualized Krishna as Rama in Vrindavan. Kabirdas (15 AD) was a devotee of Rama and composed dohas on Rama only in Brij, Awadhi and Hindi languages. Surdas a blind poet (15-16 AD) composed verses on Krishna in Brij and Awadhi languages. A Muslim named Raskan who was a devotee of Krishna composed bhajans in Brijbhasha. He translated Bhagavata Purana into the Persian language. Ravi Das (15-16 AD), a poet-saint composed verses about Krishna in Sanskrit,

Brij, Sindhi and Persian languages. His poetry was added to the Sikh scriptures, GURU GRANTH SAHIB.

SRINATHJI, NATHDWARA, RAJASTHAN

Vallabhacharya (15-16 AD) was a Telugu Brahmin who went to Kashi at a very early age, settled there as a sannyasi, and started PUSHTI MARGA (path of grace), a Vaishnava sect. He was a parivrajakacharya. He met Krishna as SHRINATHJI in Gokul when he was in teerth (pilgrim) yatra (journey). Shrinathji idol is black with a nose pin on the right side of the nose. He self-manifested from stone and emerged from Govardhan hills. When the idol was shifted from Govardhan hills to a safe place due to Muslim invasions [at Naath - Dwara (God's door) approximately 48 km from Udaipur] the chariot carrying the idol got stuck. Vallabhacharya built the temple there, considering this as God's chosen place. Vallabhacharya composed MADHURASHTAKAM. In his last days in Kashi, he could compose only 3-½ slokas in Sanskrit on the sand, on the banks of the Ganga river. The remaining 1-1/2 slokas were completed by Lord Krishna himself. These five slokas are named SHIKSHA SLOKAS. Meera Bai, queen of Mewar was a devotee of Lord Krishna from childhood. Even after marriage, she devoted herself to God only and composed kritis and bhajans on Krishna.

Chaitanya Mahaprabhu (15-16 AD) was a Bengali Krishna devotee, born in Mayapur near Navadweepa (130 km approximately from Calcutta in WB, India). He spread Krishna bhakti in the Indian subcontinent. Having travelled throughout India and learnt Vaishnavism thoroughly he established Gaudiya Vaishnavism (present-day Bengal and Bangladesh are called the Gaudiya region) in which Lord Krishna only is Supreme Being. He spread the HARE KRISHNA mantra in the Indian subcontinent. As he was spiritually powerful, he could find the important places of RadhaKrishna in Vrindavanand lived there for some time to restore them. He compiled SHISHATAKAM (8 slokas) in Sanskrit and transformed his six disciples Rupa, Sanatana, Gopala Bhatt, Raghunath Bhutt, Raghunath Das and Jeeva into goswamis to develop and spread Gaudiya Vaishnavism. Chandidas (15 AD) was a great devotee of Krishna and visualized him,. He composed 1250 verses in Bengali named SRI KRISHNA KIRTANA about RadhaKrishna bhakti philosophy based on Bhagavata Purana. According to Gaudiya Vaishnava philosophy, Krishna is self-manifested and Radha is his atma. They are not two individuals, they are one and only one. Every person in India believes this. Not only in Vrindavan, everywhere in India people worship RadhaKrishna as one. Though the RadhaKrishna philosophy is famous, Radha was not mentioned in any purana (except Harivamsa) nor in alwar's verses.

RADHAKRISHNA BHAKTI (LOVE) IS AN IMMERSION IN THE BLISS OF ALMIGHTY

But this philosophy was portrayed negatively by the compilers lately and is understood too negatively by the present generation. According to Swaminarayan philosophy, Swaminarayana (a sanyasi) was the incarnation of Lord Krishna. He described himself as RadhaKrishna in his book "SHIKSHAPATRI" in 212 verses in Sanskrit. Swaminarayana cult spread the RadhaKrishna philosophy globally. Swami Prabhupada (1896-1977 AD) a follower of Chaitya Mahaprabhu's gaudiya Vaishnavism, established ISKCON— International Society of Krishna Consciousness, and spread Krishna philosophy by HARE KRISHNA mantra globally. To fulfil the ambition of Srila Prabhupada, ISKCON, Bangalore started to build the tallest building in the world named BRUNDAVANA CHANDRODAYA MANDIR in Vrindavan in 2014, to be completed by the end of 2019.

Buddhism and Jainism both were Indian religions developed in Magadha (present-day Bihar, India), that continue to thrive in modern times. They spread from the middle-east to the south-east and far-east. Though Buddha and Mahavir (24th tirthankara of present cycle) were contemporaries, they did not meet. Rishbha dev, 1st tirthankara of Jainism travelled globally to spread Jainism. In 8th century BC Jainism spread to Nepal, Greece, Panhave (Iran), Bhali [(a city in Bactria which was north of the Hindu Kush mountains and south of Amu Darya river, covering present-day Afghanistan, Tajikistan, Uzbekistan and the northern part of Pakistan, near Russia)], Suvarnabhumi (land of gold, present day Indonesian Archipelago (an extensive group of islands) Sumatra or Java and Malaysia), Siam (present-day Thailand), Philistia (present-day Palestine), Ceylon (present-day Sri Lanka) King Ravana (in that cycle of Jainism), is said to have erected a Jain temple in Trikuta Giri and another statue of Parshwanath (unsure of number of cycle of Jainism) is found in the caves of Tripura in Sri Lanka. As Jain scriptures were in Sanskrit and Jainism spread to Russia, Russian language has more similarities with Sanskrit. Presently Jainism is not popular not only in this region but also South Asia and Far East— because of food habits. Jain food is purely vegetarian (not even egg) whereas there are no food restrictions in Buddhism. Presently Jainism is flourishing in India, USA, UK, African countries like Kenya and Uganda and is spreading fast to places like

Australia etc., as more people are migrating. Though Buddhism exists in India, it spread to Himalayan countries like Bhutan, Nepal, Tibet, Sri Lanka in the south, and then it spread to Far-Eastern countries like the Indonesian archipelago (an extensive group of islands), Malaysia, Japan and particularly China. China had adopted Buddhism because there was no religion before, only the teachings of leaders like Tao were followed and the teachings of Tao and Buddha were intermingled. Although all these countries follow Buddhism, each country has its own practitioners and set of rituals.

Though the principles of Jainism and Buddhism are based on AHIMSA, Buddhism spread fast globally in this Kali-yuga. As Lord Buddha opposed Sanskrit to encourage the vernacular (local language or dialect) dialects, his teachings were written in Pali (which was the prevailing language of the time), which was known as bootha baashaa (Paisachi baashaa). It was written on palm leaves during the fourth Buddhist council in Sri Lanka in 29 BCE, approximately 450 years after the mahasamadhi of Gautam Buddha. This Pali was written by a Sanskrit scholar and recited by a Paisachi scholar. According to some legends, Maharshi Patanjali [pata = to fall, (anjali = two palms folded together closed on one side and open on another side) who was the incarnation of Adisesha, had composed the yoga shastras in Paisachi and changed them into Sanskrit language to teach humans. As a 1000 headed snake, he descended to the earth to teach 1000 disciples at a time without any interruptions till the complete knowledge was transmitted, by putting a screen between them, and laid down a condition that if anybody interrupts in any manner, that person would be cursed to be a paisachi.

The disciples were children and curious to find out who was behind the curtain. Just when they were about to open the curtain, one boy left to answer nature's call. Once the curtain was opened, the remaining 999 boys were burnt. By the time the boy returned, the sage regretted his action. He forgave the boy for his disobedience and transmitted all the knowledge to the boy. As the boy violated rules set by maharishi, the boy was cursed to become a demon and would be relieved of the curse only when he transmitted the knowledge to some other person. The demon hung on a tree, upside down, for thousands of years waiting for a suitable disciple to whom he could transmit the knowledge. The Maharshi took pity on him and once again he was born as a human being by the name of "Chandra Verma". He became the disciple of the demon and wrote the yoga sutras on tree leaves with his blood, continuously for seven days and seven nights. As he was very tired, he fell asleep. While he was sleeping, some of the leaves fell down and were eaten by goats. The remaining leaves have given the world' Yoga Sutras' which presently we are learning and practicing. Here the language of demon [bhoot bhasha] mixed with the language of the scholar [Sanskrit] gave birth to the Pali language. Pali was written in a variety of scripts.

According to another legend, Chandra Verma, after writing continuously without any rest, was too sick to move and was taken to a hospital. There he met the daughter of the Ujjain kingdom's physician and was nursed by her [as he was unable to eat or drink, his food had to be ground into a paste and fed to him]. As per customs of the kingdom at that time he had to marry the physician's daughter. As he was very handsome, intelligent and wise, the king's daughter and the minister's daughter also wanted to marry him. According to the prevailing customs at that time, he married all the three girls. The famous king, Vikramaditya, was the son of the king's daughter, and his aide, Bhatti, was the son of the minister's daughter. After the children were born, Chandra Verma became sanyasi, left the kingdom and went to the forest to perform penance. King Vikramaditya was very intelligent and wise. With the help of his minister, Bhatti, he ruled very efficiently and he started the "Vikrama Sawant".

Lord Rama's brother, Bharata, ruled the city of Takshasila, presently called Taxila in Pakistan. Laxmana ruled Laxmana-puri, presently called Lucknow. Shatrughna ruled the forest named Madhuvana presently called Mathura. Lava, son of Lord Rama ruled present day Lahore (Pakistan) originally named Lavapuri. Present day LAOS was originally named Lavapuri after Lava. In 7th AD Kalavarnadish, King of Takshasila founded the city in Thailand named Lavapuri, presently called Lopburi which is 130 km from Bangkok. Kusha ruled the entire Kashmir valley with Kasur in Lavapuri. Present-day Cambodia's name in the Khmer language is Kampuchia which derives from the Sanskrit "Kambhojadesa". According to the inscriptions dated AD 947, an Indian sage, Swayambhuva Kambhoj. reached the peninsula and married a Naga princess, Mera, which led to the Kambuja descendants. Khmer kings ruled Cambodia from 9-15 AD and, at time of King Suryavarman II in 12 AD, ANGKOR WAT (city of temples) was built in which all the forms of Gods like Vishnu, Shiva, Krishna, Samudra Manthan etc., were sculpted in rock. Later on, it was transformed to a Buddhist temple. Even today it is the oldest, most popular destination for tourists. It is listed as UNESCO World Heritage Centre

Sage Vyasa had compiled the Mahabharata in Sanskrit. Later it was written in some Indian languages also. In the period of Mughal King Akbar, the Mahabharata was translated into Persian named RAZMNAMA (book of wars). Ramayana and Atharvaveda, Leela Ganitam (book on mathematics) were also translated into Persian. Bhagavadgita was translated into almost 80 languages (all Indian languages, European, Asian, Sinhala, Swahili, Afrikaans languages) and different dialects like Awadhi, Brij and so on. In the period of Akbar's great - grandson Dara, Bhagavadgita and Upanishads were translated by Allam Abul Faizal into Persian. The first translation of the Bhagavadgita named AL - KITA (there is no letter "GA" in Arabic) in Arabic was published in 1918 AD. Sage Vyasa had compiled Harivamsam (from Krishna's birth to Niryana). In Kurukshetra (Haryana, India) a Sri Krishna Museum was established in which all the important incidents from birth to samadhi of Lord Krishna were depicted through paintings and sculptures. Bhagavadgitas, Ramayanas in different languages and dialects in different sizes (very small to big) are stored here.

Presently, approximately 500 different Ramayanas in different languages and different dialects exist. Mostly Valmiki Ramayana, Adhyatma Ramayana, Vasistha Ramayana (yoga vasistam) in Sanskrit, Tulasidas's Ramcharitmanas in Awadhi (a dialect of Hindi) are famous. Two Ramayanas named Bhanubhakta Ramayan by Bhanubhakta Acharya in the 19th century,

Siddhi Ramayan by Siddhidas Mahaju in the 20th century were compiled in Nepali. Ramayanu was written by Krishnadasa Shama in 15th century in Konkani (Devanagiri script) language in Goa (Konkani is written in five scripts which are Devanagiri, Roman, Kannada, Malayalam, Perso - Arabic). The first English translation of Ramayana was in the 19th century by Ralph T.H. Griffith. The Urdu translation of Pothi Ramayana was written in the 17th century. As Hinduism spread to South-East Asia, some more Ramayanas were written in Reamker in Cambodia, Ramakien in Thailand, Phra Lak Phra Ram in Laos, Yama zatdaw in Burma (Myanmar), Hikayat seri Ram in Malaysia, Kakawin Ramayana in Java (Indonesia), Rajah Magandiri in Philippines. Ramacharitamanas had been translated into English in 1875 by F.S. Grouse and it was translated into Russian, German and other European languages (Book review, Hindu, Feb 2003).

As world is quite big, SUPREME BEING was incarnated in different regions in different forms with their respective set of instructions which led to different religions (Hinduism, Jainism, Buddhism, Judaism, Zoroastrianism, Taoism, Christianity, Islam etc.) and cults (Swaminarayana, ISCKON, etc.) with the same essence. In Hinduism BHAGAVADGITA played a major and important role. It has 18 chapters. Lord Krishna stated in the Bhagavadgita that he is solely responsible for good and bad deeds of every living, non-living being.

As the number "18" has great importance in Indian Mythology,

Bhagavan VED VYAS had written

1. Ashtadasa (18) puranas

2. Ashtadasa (18) upa-puranas

3. 108 (18 × 6) Upanishads (presently 19 exist)

4. Mahabharata epic is written "18" sargas (sarga = part)

5. In Mahabharata "18" lakh words were written

6. Kurukshetra war was fought for "18" days (One hour in Dwapara-yuga is equal to two hours in Kali-yuga yuga)

7. War was fought with army of "18" Akshauhinis [Kauravas had 11 akshauhinis and Pandavas had 7 akshauhinis]

Akshauhini is an army consisting of 21, 870 raths; 21, 870 elephants; 65, 610 cavalry (soldiers on horseback) and 109, 350 infantry (soldiers marching on foot). Add up all the digits in each category and they will come to "18".

Lord Krishna narrated the "Bhagavad Gita" to Arjuna on the beginning of the first day of Mahabharata war which has "18" chapters. On the advice of Lord Krishna, Bheeshma pitamaha narrated the "Vishnu Sahasranamam" [1000 names in praise of Lord Vishnu in 108 = 6×18 slokas] on the end of the 18th day of war to King Yuddhistira (Dharma Raja). Lord Krishna narrated 1000 names of Lord Shiva which he learnt from Sage Upamanyu to Dharma Raja. In Ashwamedha parva when Arjuna requested Lord Krishna to repeat Bhagavadgita, Lord narrated the same in brief as ANUGITA. In another epic, Ramayana, the war between Rama and Ravana was fought for "18" days (One hour in Treta-yuga is equal to three hours in Kali-yuga).

Krishna narrates in the Bhagavadgita:

Sanskrit Transliteration:

परित्राणाय साधूनां विनाशाय च दुष्कृताम्।

धर्मसंस्थापनार्थाय सम्भवामि युगे युगे॥

English Transliteration:

Paritraanaaya saaduunaam vinaashaayacha dushkrutaam |

Dharmasamsthaanaaya sambhavaami yuge yuge ||

In this sloka Lord Krishna explained to the devotees through Arjuna that whenever, wherever, however they need, he will rescue them.

Sanskrit Transliteration:

पत्रं पुष्पं फलं तोयं यो मे भक्त्या प्रयच्छति।

तदहं भक्त्युपहृतमश्नामि प्रयतात्मन: ॥

English Transliteration:

Patram pushpam phalam toyam yo me bhaktya prayacchathi |

Tadaham bhaktyuprahrutam ashnami prayataatmanaha ||

In this sloka Lord Krishna explained to the devotees through Arjuna that whoever offers anything (patram = leaf, pushpam = flower, phalam = fruit, toyam = water) with bhakti, he will appear in Saguna Rupa and consume it.

LORD KRISHNA IS BHAKTI, RAKTI (PLEASANTNESS), MUKTI.

Conclusion:

Sets of instructions delivered orally by the SUPREME BEING in Hinduism, Buddhism and Jainism were mostly written on the medium of Tala-Patra (tada or tala means cured palm, patra means leaf) used in Southeast Asia from 5 BC to 19 AD. They were transcribed onto paper (19-20 AD). Presently they are transmitted through computers and should be transmitted to future generations through the medium available at that time.

It is a continuous process.

PILGRIMAGE TO HIMALAYAN MOUNTAIN RANGE–AN EXPERIENCE

Geographically, the Himalayas are the youngest mountain ranges in the world and they have the third largest deposits of ice and snow in the world after Antarctica and the Arctic. The Indian plateau took approximately a 6000 km journey before its collision with Eurasian plateau (Asia). Present-day Indian Plateau is approximately 10 million years

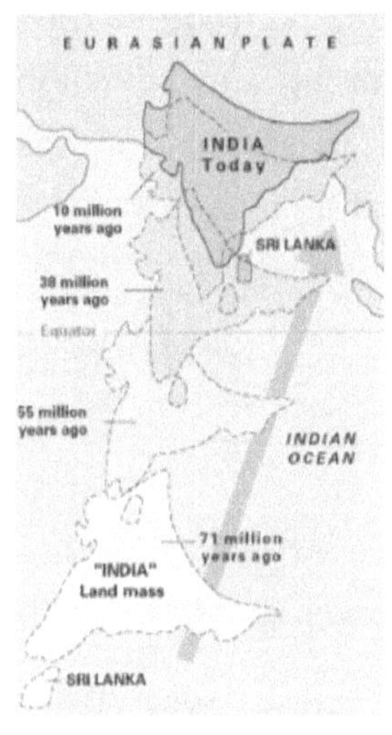

old. The world's major rivers like the Indus, the Ganges, the Tsangpo - Brahmaputra which are perennial, rise in the Himalayas.

Himalayas are the mountain range stretching from Karakoram in Pakistan to Arunachal Pradesh in India. The range passes through Jammu and Kashmir (India), Himachal Pradesh (India), Uttarakhand (India), Tibet, Nepal, Sikkim in India, Bhutan and ends at Arunachal Pradesh in India. We have visited the Himalayan ranges from Kashmir to Sikkim in the span of 30 years. Himalayas are snow-clad mountains. (In Sanskrit, "Hima" means snow and "alaya" means dwelling. Himalaya means "abode of snow".) The Himalayas separate the Indian subcontinent from the Tibetan Plateau, and are also called South Asia mountains which shaped the cultures of South Asia. The Himalayan peaks are sacred to Buddhists, Hindus and Jains.

INDIA MAP

The importance of these religions and places in relation to Himalayan range is discussed in this article. A brief view on these three religions and my experience of this pilgrimage is given below.

God is Unique, Energy, Omnipotent, Omnipresent. God manifests in different forms which lead to different religions and cults. Hinduism, Buddhism, Jainism flourished in the Himalayan mountain region extensively.

HIMALAYAN MOUNTAINS

Buddhism: Siddhartha Gauthama [the prince of the Kapilavasthu (Sakhya capital), India in 4th to 5th BC] obtained ENLIGHTENMENT in Bodh Gaya

LORD BUDDHA

PRAYER FLAGS

(in present-day Bihar, India) under the BODH (peepal) tree. As 'Buddha' means 'Enlightened one' it is used to describe the first awakened being in an ERA. Siddhartha was named 'Gauthama Buddha', and it is on his teachings that Buddhism is founded. The time of his birth and mahasamadhi (death) are uncertain. Buddhism spread from present day AFGHANISTAN through the complete Himalayan Mountain Range to China, Far East and Japan. Buddhism's main principle is 'AHIMSA'. The BUDDHA leads us to 'ENLIGHTENMENT'— manifesting in the form of the mantra 'OM MANI PADME HUM'. It is a six-syllable Sanskrit mantra, where Mani means 'Jewel' or 'Bead', Padma means 'Lotus Flower'. It is hard to understand the mantra and it is not easy to translate it into other languages. The Dalai Lama explained that 'Mantra'

ॐमणिपद्मेहूँ

औँमणिपद्मेहूँ

ᰍᰕᰓᰦᰎᰉᰔᰴᰒ

ཨོཾ་མ་ཎི་པ་དྨེ་ཧཱུྃ

ཨོཾ་མ་ཎི་པ་དྨེ་ཧཱུྃ།

ཨོཾ་མ་ཎི་པད་མེ་ཧཱུྃ།

means one can transform one's impure body, speech and mind into the body, speech and mind of Buddha.

PRAYER WHEELS

The mantra is commonly painted or carved on rocks, on paper and on yak skulls. Paper with the mantra written on it is inserted into a 'Prayer Wheel' and, when an individual spins the wheel, the effect is the same as reciting the mantra. Prayer Wheels vary in size and type. Some are handheld wheels which are made of hollow wooden or metal cylinders attached to a handle. In the Himalayan Mountain Range, one finds the Tibetan Buddhists turning the wheel while walking or resting, murmuring the mantra. All the Buddhist monasteries have bucket-sized prayer wheels lined upon wooden racks along walking paths

ASTAPAD

encircling the main shrine. People commonly find the prayer flags, which are made of cotton cloth in white, blue, red, yellow and green with mantras and prayers written on them, in the mountain ranges. Jainism: The origins of Jainism are obscure (unknown). Jains believe their religion to be ever existing having no origin and end. It is occasionally forgotten by humans and revived by a succession of tirthankaras. Ashtapad (in Sanskrit "ashta" means eight and "pad" means steps)

is one of the major Jain teerthas and is situated in the snow-covered Himalayas which is approximately 7 km away from Manasasarover on the way to Mt. Kailash. Here Bhagavan Rishabhdev [also called Bhagavan Adinath] attained enlightenment [nirvana]. He was the founder of Jainism in the present half-cycle of time. His son, King Bharat, after Rishabdev's salvation, established the Ashdapad temple as a palace of real gemstones with idols [made of gemstones] of the 24 tirthankaras in the Ashtapad mountains [near Mt. Kailash]. Jainism's main principle is 'AHIMSA'.

Hinduism: Hinduism is the oldest religion in the world and it is the dominant religion in Southeast Asia, mostly in India. Hindu temples, Buddhist monasteries and

Jain temples were established in the Himalayan Mountain Ranges from Afghanistan to Arunachal Pradesh via Tibet and Nepal. According to Hinduism, God manifested into many different forms like Lord

Shiva, Lord Vishnu, etc. Hindus chant different mantras using a garland of beads (Japa = mantra, mala = garland). Madhaviya Shankara Vijayam states that pre-existing Sarvajnanapeetha in Kashmir (Sharada Peetham) had four doors for scholars from four directions. The southern door was never opened until Adi Shankara visited in the early 8th century and defeated all the scholars in all the branches of Hindu philosophy. Presently Sharada Peetham is also called the Saraswati temple which is one of the Shakti Peethas of 18 maha Shakti Peethas and it is in Azad Kashmir (Pakistan-Occupied -Kashmir).

SHANKARA HILLS

Kashmir: Kashmir is a historical settlement which dates back to pre-Mahabharata and is part of the oldest major civilizations. As per the folk legend from Hindu mythology, "Kashmir" means "desiccated land" and in Sanskrit, "Ka" means water and "shimeera" means desiccated; it was formerly a lake and was drained by Sage Kashyap, grandson of Lord Brahma. In the Mahabharata period, the Khambojas ruled Kashmir, later the Panchalas ruled the same. The present day Peer Panjal range was named after the Panchalas and prefixed with a Muslim word "peer" in memory of a Muslim fakir. Buddhism was developed in Srinagari (present-day Srinagar), which was the capital of Kashmir in the Mauryan period, by the Mauryan emperor, King Ashoka. Buddhist monks from central and east Asia used to visit Kashmir. The Kuchanese

AMARNATH LINGAM

monk Kumarajiva (born to an Indian family) spread Buddhism to China. The Amarnath cave, where a shivling is formed by an ice stalagmite, lies in the snow-clad mountains and is about 140 km from Srinagar. It is a very sacred pilgrimage centre for Hindus and is open in the months of July and August. Adi Shankaracharya temple, also called Shankara hills, is situated on a hill near Srinagar. It is dedicated to Lord Shiva and is named "Jyoteshwar" temple.

VISHNAVI MATA

VAISHNAVI MATA (Jammu): Ma Vaishnavidevi who is one of the 108 Shaktipeethas, is situated in Katra near Jammu. Hindu mythology says that 52 parts of Goddess Sati fell to the earth, 56 fell on the other planets. Out of these, the "blessing hand" of Goddess Sati fell on the planet Venus or Shukra Graha, which was abode of Goddess Lakshmi. In early Treta-yuga, the demon, Mura, blessed with boons by Lord Brahma, chased Lord Vishnu onto the planet Shukra.

After watching the chase for a long time, Adiparashakti (Goddess of The Universe), on the request of Goddess Lakshmi, took the form of Kaali in the physical appearance of the girl with the soul of Goddess Lakshmi and Goddess Saraswati (knowledge), named "Kumari". As the demon chased Lord Vishnu, Lord Shiva shifted the mountain from Shukra to the Himalayas on earth. While chasing Lord Vishnu, Mura (the demon) was obstructed by Kumari who helped Lord Vishnu kill the demon; hence Lord Vishnu is named "Murari". All the three Goddesses transformed into pindies (sacred stones).

Another legend says that Goddess Lakshmi, named "Trikuta" by sage Narada, was incarnated as a daughter of Lord Ratnakara. Trikuta is also called Vaishnavi who performed penance to unite with Lord Rama (Lord Rama is the incarnation of Lord Vishnu). In the incarnation as Lord Rama, the Lord could have only one wife. As Lord Rama could not marry Vaishnavi, the Lord asked her to set up an ashram in the Trikuta hills of the Himalayas, meditate, and wait till the end of Kali-yuga. Vaishnavi shred her physical form and transformed into a five-foot rock with three heads of pindies (sacred stones). The temple contains three idols of Maha Saraswati, Maha Lakshmi, Maha Kaali— together they form Vaishnavi Mata.

RAGHUNATH TEMPLE

In the heart of Jammu city exists the famous "Raghunath Temple" which was built in the 19th century by Maharaja Gulab Singh and his son Maharaja Ranbeer Singh. The presiding deity of the temple is Lord Rama after whom the temple is named. It is one of the largest temple complexes in North India with seven shrines, each with its own shikhara. The significance of the temple

LADAKH

is the idols of planets (Surya, Sukra, etc.), celestial bodies (Indra, Varuna, etc.), important personalities (Dhanwantari, Charaka, etc.), Gods (Shiv, Parvathi. etc.), Lord Satyanarayana Swamy (Skanda Purana, Revakande) were installed. Important temples like Char Dham, Jyotirlingas were built. Ladakh is a part of Jammu and Kashmir, whose capital is Leh. Buddhism flourished here. Even now Ladakhis follow Buddhism.

Himachal Pradesh: Himachal Pradesh is also a state in the Himalayas, its capital is Shimla. This state is blessed with five Shaktipeethas. They are Chintpurni temple in Una district, Chamunda, Jwala, Brijeshwari temple in Kangra district, Naina Devi temple in Bilaspur district.

HIMACHAL PRADESH

Historically, this part of the region was ruled by the Gupta dynasty from the 4th to 6th century. This period is called "the Golden Age of India" and is marked by invention and discoveries in science, mathematics, technology, engineering, art, logic, literature, dialects, astronomy, religion, philosophy. This period produced scholars like Kalidasa, Aryabhatta, Varahamihira, Vatsayana, Vishnu Sharma and Amarasimha. Amarasimha had written a thesaurus in Sanskrit called Amarakosha. King Harshavardhana ruled this region after defeating the Guptas in the 6th century. The court poet, Bana, the Chinese traveller, Xuantsang, and the great mathematician and astronomer, Brahmagupta, lived here. In this period both Buddhism and Hinduism flourished. There are many important monasteries.

DEV BHOOMI (UTTARAKHAND): Uttarakhand is called the "abode of Gods" (Dev Bhoomi). Adi Shankaracharya had established temples in Kedarnath (Jyotirlinga) and in Badrinath (Nara Narayana), which are in the heart of the Himalayas. The great poet Kalidasa praised the Himalayas in his great epic "Kumara Sambhavam".

KUMARASAMBHAVAM CANTOS 1 TO 7 BY M.R. KALE.

This sloka is the FIRST SLOKA from the first canto and is on the first page.

ASTUTTARASYAM DISHI DEVATHABHYAM, HIMALAYONAMA NAGHADHIRAJAH

POORVAPARAU TOYA NIDHEE VAGAAHYA, STHITHAH PRUTHIVYA IVA MAANADANDAH.

Meaning of the sloka is: There is in the northern quarter, the deity-soul "Lord of mountains" (immovable), by the name "THE HIMALAYAS" (the mountains of snow), who stands measuring of earth, spanning the eastern and western oceans: Allasani Peddanna, one of the eight court poets (Ashta diggajalu, diggajamu = elephant, means eight court poets are powerful and great as an elephant)

BHADRINATH

patronized by the great King Sri Krishnadevaraya of Vijayanagara empire during 15th century, described the Himalayas in his book, MANUCHARITRA, as: "Snow-clad mountains so beautiful, they look like their high peaks are touching the sky." According to the Mahabharata, after the great KURUKSHETRA war, fought between the Kauravas and Pandavas, the

Pandavas wanted to absolve the sins of killing their kith and kin. They left for the darshan of Lord Shiva in Mt. Kailash. Enroute, the Pandavas found a place called Kashi, where Lord Shiva was hiding. Hence the name 'Gupta (hidden) Kashi'. After travelling for some time they reached a place called 'Gauri Kund' (base camp for Kedarnath). According to the Shivapurana (epic), Goddess Parvati (Gauri) is believed to have performed penance for her union with Lord Shiva in this Himalayan region. Hence the name Gauri Kund. From there they travelled to a place called Kedar (this region was ruled by King Kedar in the Treta-yuga). Here Lord Shiva appeared as a Jyothirlinga from a huge column of light. Hence Lord is named 'KEDARESHWARA'. From there, the Pandavas travelled to Badrinath (Badarikashrama), where sages like Nara, Narayana, Sanaka, Sanandana performed penance from time immemorial. Even now sadhus perform penance here. From here the Pandavas travelled to Mt. Kailash.

BHAGIRATHI

The sacred rivers like Mandakini (also called AAKAASHA GANGA), Alaknanda, Bhagirathi, the mystic Saraswati, Yamuna, etc., flow perennially from the Himalayas. From the puranas (Shivapurana, Skandapurana), we conclude that this region might be the birth place of Lord Subramanya. The puranas say that King Baghiratha, anxious to release his ancestors' souls (60 thousand sons of King Sagara), performed

BRAHMA KAMAL

rigorous penance and was granted the prize of Ganga's descent from heaven. King Bhagiratha persuaded Lord Shiva on Mt. Kailash to receive Ganga in his coils of tangled hair, as her turbulence could shatter the earth. As Lord Shiva releases Ganga, she flows from the mouth of Gomukh to Gangotri (It

GURUDWARA,
HEMA KUND

is named as Bhagirathi in honour of Bhagiratha and meets Alaknanda, Mandakini, Pindar, Nandakini (Alaknanda meets Bhagirathi in Devprayag, Pindar in Karnaprayag, Nandakini in Nandaprayag, Mandakini in Rudraprayag, Dauli ganga in Vishnuprayag: panch '5' Prayag:), flows to Rishikesh. From there she flows as the River Ganges, travels through Allahabad, Varanasi, Gaya, meets the ocean (Bay of Bengal) and flows deep into the netherworld (patalam), saving King Sagara's sons.

In the Garhwal-Himalayan range lies Hemkund lake and Gurudwara (sacred to Sikhs). Down the lake, lies the Valley of Flowers, where a variety of flowers grow, some of which are sacred (Brahma-Kamal)

MAYAVATHI

and medicinal (Brahma-Kamal, Sanjeevini herb, etc.). In Mayawati near Almora (Kumaon Himalayan range), Swamy Vivekananda established an Advaita ashram in 1899. No images or idols are kept in the ashram. The ashram is dedicated to the study and practice of the Advaita Vedanta (Atma is Brahman and vice-versa), and the rules were set by Swami Vivekananda.

KAILASH-MANASASAROVER: Mt. Kailash and Manasasarover are sacred places for Hindus, Buddhists and Jains, and are mentioned in the Rigveda (I have not visited personally, but gathered information from friends who visited). Swamy Pranavananda said that the lake is the holiest, most fascinating, most inspiring, most famous of all the lakes in the world and the most ancient, any

Mt. KAILASH

civilization has known. Skandapurana states that, "There are no mountains like Mt. Kailash and no lake like Manasasarover in the Himalayan mountains. Just as how the dew is dried up by the morning sun, so are the sins of mankind dried up by the sight of the Himalayas." A pilgrimage to Mt. Kailash for Hindus, Buddhists, and Ashtapaad near the south face of Mt. Kailash for Jains, is very sacred. Mt. Kailash is described as the centre of universe in Hindu puranas, Buddhist texts, Ashtapaad in Jain texts, Yungdrung - Tseg (nine storey swastika mountain) in Bonpa tradition (Tibetan Buddhism). For Hindus, Mt. Kailash is the abode of Lord Shiva and Goddess Parvathi. For Jains, Mt. Kailash is the site where their first tirthankar achieved NIRVANA (ENLIGHTENMENT). For the ancient religion of Bon, (Tibetan Buddhism), it is where the founder' Guru Padmasambhava' descended from heaven. The legend according to the Tibetan tradition is that whenever a certain number of realized beings (Buddhist saints) gather together in this location, Lord Gautham Buddha manifests there.

MANASASAROVERRR

Manasasarovar is created by Lord Brahma's manas (hriday). It is the largest freshwater lake in the world, and it is almost perfectly circular; its circumference is approximately 90 kms. As Hindu scriptures say, bathing in this lake and drinking its water cleanses all the sins. Buddhists believe that this lake is the legendary lake, ANAVATAPTA, in Sanskrit and ANATOTTA in Pali, where queen Maya is believed to have conceived Lord Buddha. Hindus believe that celestial bodies (Sidda, Yaksha, Kinnera, Kimpurusha, Gandharva, Vidyadhara, etc.) who cannot be seen by the human eye, float down from sky, take a dip in the lake and float upwards. (Mysterious lights 2012, YouTube). Mt. Everest is known as SAGARMATHA in Nepal, and is the earth's highest mountain. In the northern slopes of Mt. Everest, Guru Padmasambhava (lotus-born) established a monastery in Rongchuk dedicated to Tibetan Buddhism. We had a view of Mt. Everest from the Kathmandu flight.

JALAKSHAYANA NARAYANA

KATHMANDU: Kathmandu is a land of significant temples of which one is Pashupatinath, Sleeping Vishnu temple. The temple is the oldest Hindu temple which is on the banks of the river Bagmati, and it is one of the 275 holy abodes of Lord Shiva on the continent. Pashupathinath means Lord Shiva is the Lord of all pashus (living and non-living

PASUPATINATH

beings). The Shiva Linga is four-headed which dates back to 400 AD. Near the temple there is a shaktipeeth "Guhyeshwari" , which is one of the 52 shaktipeethas spread over South Asia and is very near the Bagmati river. The Budhikanta statue (Jalakshayana Narayana)

PADMASAMBHAVA, BUDDHISM

lying in a reclining position inside a recessed water tank (representing cosmic sea or ocean of milk), on the twisting coils of Adisesha (1000-headed snake: King of Serpent deities) is the largest and most beautiful carving in Nepal. Boudhanath (Stupa) in Kathmandu is the largest stupa in the world and dominates the skyline. Its construction is based on Padmasambhava Buddhism (Tibetan) and was built just after the mahasamadhi of Lord Buddha. Its stupa is adorned by many kilos of gold, and it is the largest single Chhyorten (Buddhist shrine) in the world.

CHYORTEN, KHATMANDU, NEPAL

SIKKIM: Kanchenjunga Himal is a range of the Himalayas and is located in eastern Nepal and in Sikkim (India). Kanchenjunga is the second highest peak in Nepal and the third highest in the world. The local meaning of Kanchenjunga is "five treasures of high snow", which represents the five repositories of God, and they are gold, silver, gems, food grain and religious texts. Kanchenjunga is seen from Gangtok

BABA

(capital of Sikkim), Pelling (Sikkim), Kalimpong (West Bengal), Tiger valley: Darjeeling (West Bengal). On the way to Nathula Pass (silk route) a sacred lake, Tsomgo (12,400 ft) and at Nathula, Baba Mandir are visible. Major (BABA) Harbhajan Singh (Punjabi) was an Indian army soldier who died at the age of 25, in the Indo-China war near Nathula Pass. He is revered by soldiers of the Indian army who built a shrine in his honour. He is called the Hero of Nathula. Every soldier feels that Baba's spirit saves them; Baba grants them favours.

THATHAGHAT

A Tibetan Buddhist saint, Padmasambhava, also known as Guru Rinchope, introduced Buddhism in the 8th century in Sikkim. The tallest statue of saint Padmasambhava in the world is established on "SAMDRUPTSE HILL" (wish-fulfilling hill) close to Namchi (Sikkim). Buddha Park in Rabong (Sikkim) was opened in 2013 to commemorate the 2550 birth anniversary of Lord Buddha. It features a 130 ft tall statue of Lord Buddha as its centrepiece. Inside the cylindrical complex, the life of Buddha (from birth to samadhi) is painted in colour, and the park is called "THATHAGATH TSAL". Bhutan, Arunachal Pradesh (India) [not visited] are in eastern end of the Himalayas. Buddhism is the main religion in Bhutan. Big monasteries have been built here around the 17th century. Arunachal Pradesh means "Land of dawn-lit mountains", and it is in the border between China and India. Legend says that the Hindu texts, Kalki Purana and Mahabharata mention the region as the "Prabhu mountains" of the puranas.

The Himalayas are most important and sacred for Hindus, Buddhists and Jains. Let us pray to God that they remain sacred forever.

MY PILGRIMAGE TO KEDARNATH AND BADRINATH

Badrinath and Kedarnath, the abode of Gods and immortals, with their legends and fascinating stories, holds a thrilling experience for one and all. We went on a pilgrimage to Kedarnath and Badrinath. There we observed some interesting facts based on legends from the epics, Mahabharata and Ramayana. I want to share my views on the significance of the section of Himalayas stretching from Kedarnath to Almora in Uttarakhand which is believed to be the land of Gods.

After the great Mahabharata war in Kurukshetra, the Pandavas wanted to absolve themselves of the sins of killing their relatives; they wanted to worship Lord Shiva. After installing their grandson, Parikshith, [son of Uttara and Abhimanyu (son of Arjuna and Subhadra)] as King of Hastinapur, they left on a pilgrimage to seek the blessings of Lord Shiva. As Lord Shiva was away in Mt. Kailash in Himalayas, the Pandavas left for the Himalayas via Haridwar and Rishikesh. On the way, they saw Lord Shiva from a distance. But Lord Shiva hid from them. Then

Dharamraj, eldest of Pandavas, named that place as Gupta Kashi. From Gupta Kashi they went ahead to the place called Gaurikund.

According to Shivapurana, Goddess Parvati performed penance for her union with Lord Shiva in this Himalayan region, hence the name Gaurikund. There are some hot springs near Gaurikund which is the base camp for the Kedarnath temple. There Bheema (the second brother of Pandavas) and his brothers found a bull which had a unique look. As it was running away from them. Bheema went after the bull with his mace and attacked the animal ferociously. The bull hid its face in a deep hole in the earth. In the tug of war between Beema and the bull, the face of the bull was dragged to Nepal, the hind part remained in a place called Kedar, named after King Kedar who ruled in Satya (Kruta) yuga. This hind part transformed into a jyotirlinga and Lord Shiva emanated from the huge column of light. By getting the darshan of the Lord, the Pandavas were absolved of their sins. Lord Shiva proclaimed that he would be visible in a triangular-shaped form. Hence the place is called Kedarnath and the Lord himself is called Kedareshwara. In the sanctum sanctorum the Lord is worshipped in a rough conical formation. In the main hall we can view the installed statues of the Pandavas, Lord Krishna, Nandi, Draupadi, Veerabhadra, etc.

In this enchanting Himalayan range in Uttarakhand, lies Badarikashrama (an abode of peace). It is a sacred place where, from time immemorial, Hindu sages like Nara and Narayana (Krishna and Arjuna of Dwapara-yuga) performed severe penance. Another legend says that Narayana performed penance under the Badri tree (this tree is a form of Goddess Lakshmi). Nara and Narayana requested Lord Shiva to settle down on the other side of Badarikashrama. Then Lord Shiva incarnated as Kedareswara Jyotirlinga. Great sages like Sanaka, Sanandana (immortal) too performed penance in Badarikashrama. Even now many sadhus perform penance there. It is believed that in the 8th century. Adi Shankara revived the temples in Kedarnath and Badrinath in Badarikashrama and attained mahasamadhi in Kedarnath. It is believed that Adi Shankara established four shankara maths in four corners of India, the one in north is in Joshimath near Badrinath.

After having the darshan of Lord Shiva, the Pandavas set out for Badarikashrama, and then they travelled to Mana village [the source of the mystic river, Saraswati, which later disappears from the land surface and is believed to flow as an undercurrent (antharvahini). It joins with Ganga and Yamuna at Allahabad at the Triveni Sangamam (the point of confluence of three rivers)]. From there they move to Vasundhara falls and, after passing through Mana Pass they reached Mt. Kailash and Manasasarover.

It is believed that in 1929 Swami Tapovanam, having learnt from the puranas that Lord Krishna and several great rishis took the same path to visit Lord Shiva in Mt. Kailash and Manasasarover lake, walked all the way with his entourage bearing severe hardships. By moving around Badrinath and Mana village, we perceived that the same route might have been taken by the Pandavas to reach Mt. Kailash. In the Himalayan range where Badrinath temple is situated, lies the Hemkund lake. In the Mahabharata period this part of Himalayan range was called Ganmadhana hills; presently it is called Garhwal-Himalayan range. Lower down lies the Valley of Flowers. It is believed that Guru Gobind Singh took a holy dip in Hema Kund and performed penance there. The Sikhs built a gurudwara there. This gurudwara is sacred to the Sikh community and Sikhs from all over the world take a pilgrimage to this gurudwara from May to November.

In the Himalayan range extending from Badrinath to the Valley of Flowers, lies the place where the famous Brahma Kamal grows. This is the flower created by Lord Brahma to help Lord Shiva place the head of an elephant on the body of the Lord Ganesha. The flower dropped the Amruta (the elixir of life) from its petals on the body. Hence the white lotus is named Brahma Kamal and has medicinal value and is used extensively in Ayurveda. This flower had an interesting anecdote in Mahabharata. During the Pandavas'stay in Kamyaka forest (12 years of exile), Draupadi felt uneasy and restless one day. Some time later she came in touch with this flower flowing downstream. After holding the flower Draupadi felt easy and happy. Then she appealed to Bhima to go in search and bring her the flower. Bheema swam upstream for some time and came face to face with Lord Hanuman near Hemkund lake.

The Sanjeevini herb which revived Lakshmana (brother of Lord Rama), brought by Hanuman to Lanka is from the Dunagiri hill in the Himalayas near Almora, which is near the Hemakund lake. The Valley of Flowers stretches from Govindghat to Almora. As Lord Hanuman is believed to be chiranjeevi (immortal), locals believe that he stays there and roams around in the Himalayan mountain ranges. Ashwatthama (immortal), who was transformed into a Paishachi through curse of Lord Krishna for using a Brahmastram to kill the child in the womb of Uttara (wife of Abhimanyu), roams in these mountains. Veda Vyasa (immortal), author of Ashtadasa puranas and the Mahabharata (Panchama Veda) meditates in these mountains. Muchikunda Maharshi (once king) was commander-in-chief for the Devatas before Lord Subramanya was born (might have been in chakshusha manvantara as Lord Shiva married Parvati in beginning of Vaivasvata manvantara and Subramanya was born on the same gandhamadhana mountains), lived through so many yugas and killed King Kalayavana on the command of Lord Krishna in the caves of Ananthagiri hills in the Deccan plateau near Hyderabad (Telangana state) in the present Dwapara-yuga of 28th Chatur-yuga of Vaivasvata (7) manvantara. Seeing the darshan of Lord Krishna, Muchikunda's eyes filled with water, which flowed as a river called Muchikunda River, which later changed to Musi River. He was blessed by the Lord to live till the end of Kali-yuga of 28th Chatur-yuga. He is presently believed to be living and meditating in the caves of these mountains.

The Land of Uttarakhand (abode of Gods) which has several more pilgrimage centres, played an important role in the Mahabharata and Ramayana is sure to play an even more important role even in the present and future of India.

THE END

EPILOGUE

As the articles are based on puranas and temples, the process of creation, maintenence, destruction is continuous process. The cycle repeats.

www.ingramcontent.com/pod-product-compliance
Lightning Source LLC
Chambersburg PA
CBHW022027150726
47990CB00002B/851